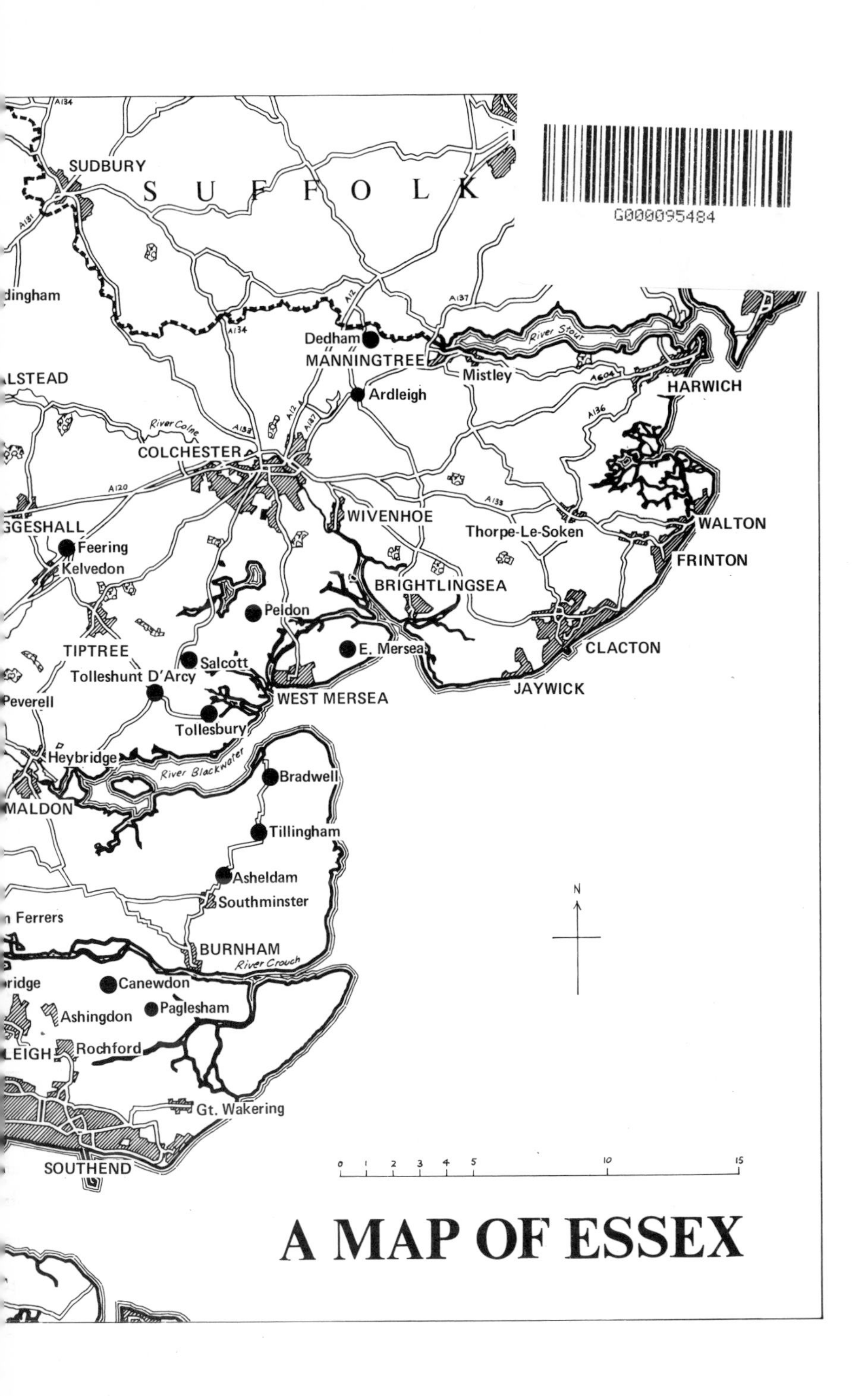

A MAP OF ESSEX

ESSEX CURIOSITIES

A History of the Old, Odd and Unusual in Essex

Other Titles by the same author

OF DOGS AND DUTY
LEISURE IN ESSEX
WAR MEDALS
COLLECTING MILITARIA

ESSEX CURIOSITIES

A History of the Old, Odd and Unusual in Essex

by

DEREK E. JOHNSON

SPURBOOKS LIMITED

Published by
SPURBOOKS LTD.
1 Station Road,
Bourne End,
Buckinghamshire.

S B N 0 902875 46 9

ACKNOWLEDGEMENTS

Firstly my thanks to all those who, when they heard I had started work on this project came forward with news of relevant places, objects and interesting items. Without them my task would have been even more exacting.

Next, the Reference Librarian and his staff of Clacton Public Library, the curator and staff of Colchester Castle Museum, and Leslie Bichener, editor of *Essex Countryside.*

Additional photographs were supplied by my good friends, Ray Shaw, Stan Shelley, Ron Wigley, Kerford-Byrnes, Ken Adams, Tony Ray and the late Leslie Cole.

Last, but by no means least, my thanks to my wife Chick, who during the long summer months has acted (uncomplainingly!) as my chauffeur.

Contents

ILLUSTRATIONS

INTRODUCTION

Essex Curiosities

The county of Essex with its mixture of towns, villages and seaside watering places has many unseen qualities. Unseen that is until you start to search in and around the most unlikely places, for there are to be found items, objects and places that rightly earn the title of curiosities.

Within these pages the reader will be taken on a strange journey, into graveyards, churches, barns, windmills, and to old inns. Not all the subjects are sombre, many have a touch of human failure and humour, for this is truly life and the way that it ticks. Strange are the stories that revolve around the south door of the church at Runwell as can be seen in the account of Rainaldus and his fatal clash with the Devil, while who would have dreamt of a complete windmill being transported from one village to the next perched on the back of a horse and cart! Stocks, lock-ups and whipping-posts synonymous with those good old days of rough justice and instant punishment still linger on, preserved as rustic relics and for those awarded more stringent measures, the dank dungeons of Colchester Castle must have struck terror into the very soul of those awaiting transportation or execution.

On the lighter side we have the strange little hatch in Foulkbourne Post Office, evidence of a sleepy postmaster, while the Maypole at Tolleshunt D'Arcy can conjure up ghosts and spirits of long forgotten rites when lads and lasses danced away through to early morning welcoming Spring with all its fringe benefits.

To those new to the county of Essex I hope this book will prove enlightening, while for those true "Essex Calves" I hope it will serve as a constant source of reference and entertainment.

With the face of our countryside always changing under the label of progress, some of the places and objects covered in this work may well have been removed by the time of publication. If this is the case I would deem it a great favour to learn about it.

A point of interest in passing, for those who feel that Princess Pocahontas is trespassing, I should point out that as she died on the Essex side of the river I thought it only fitting that she should be included!

Derek E. Johnson.

CHAPTER I

Clocks, Bells, Hour-Glasses, Gates, Weathervanes, Sundials

Come hail, rain or shine, war or peace, the old Town Hall, church, and village clocks seem to tick on taking everything in their stride. If they could only talk and recount the times gone-by what stirring tales they could tell. Of days when horseless carriage and flying machine did not exist, and the pace of living was slow and leisurely with time to think and relax.

As time slipped by it became common to replace the old hand-forged time-pieces with more modern mechanisms, but luckily for us a few do still exist to be listed as curios. One of the oldest clocks in Essex is that to be found built into the south tower of the parish church of St. Leonard-at-the-Hythe. The clock-face of stone circa 1500 with circular dial has radiating figures and carved spandrels.

Another fine example is the Clock House, Great Dunmow, which is rated as late 16th or early 17th century. Built into an octagonal cupola the clock is accompanied by a bell inscribed, "Bryan Eldridge, 1651". The pretty village of Felsted, just 5½ miles from Braintree, has a number of medieval monuments among them being the parish church of the Holy Cross, which stands on the north side of the village, where the clock, dated 1701, also carries an inscription on the works . . . *"Johannes Fordham De Dunmow Magna Fecit Anno 1701 Num 126".*

The clock mounted on Leyton parish church originally came from Leyton Great House which was demolished in 1806, while the Saxon tower of St. Andrew's Minster boasts a commemorative timepiece installed after the death of Edward VII in 1910.

At Ingatestone Hall, now serving as the Essex Records Office, a fine 18th century, blue enamelled, one-handed clock can be seen. It bears the motto Sans Dieu Rien ("Without God, nothing").

One-handed clock, Ingatestone Hall

On April 22nd 1884 Colchester was rocked by an earthquake. Hundreds of dogs ran barking through the streets and horses stampeded in fright. A tram standing at North Hill railway station was rocked so violently from side to side that the driver was pitched head-first from his cab on to the line. There appears to have been no fatal injuries, although a large number of folk suffered minor cuts and bruises and over one thousand houses were so badly damaged that they had to be completely rebuilt. St. Peter's church, North Hill, also suffered, for the central tower was so weakened that the clock had to be remounted on a stone wall bracket which can still be seen to this day.

The rather plain clock on the village hall at Great Holland was formerly of great use to the villagers. Around the turn of the century the building was used as the village baths. Purchasing a brass sixpenny token from the local Post Office the locals would queue for a weekly dip, and woe-betide those who went over their allotted time, for the old clock was watched closely by the others awaiting their turn.

Closely associated with clocks are, of course, bells. Visitors to the historic little church of St. Catherine at East Tilbury, standing close to the River Thames, will see the bell cast by William Oldfield in 1629, mounted upright beneath a catherine-wheel candelabrum near the 400 year old font. The original bell tower was destroyed by cannon shot from the river in 1667 when Tilbury was raided by the Dutch.

A strange practice is carried out at the church of Great Bromley where the hat of the captain of the bell-ringers is dated and hung high in the belfry on his death. No one knows when this ritual began, but the oldest hat there is some 257 years old.

Hats belonging to Captains of Bell-ringers

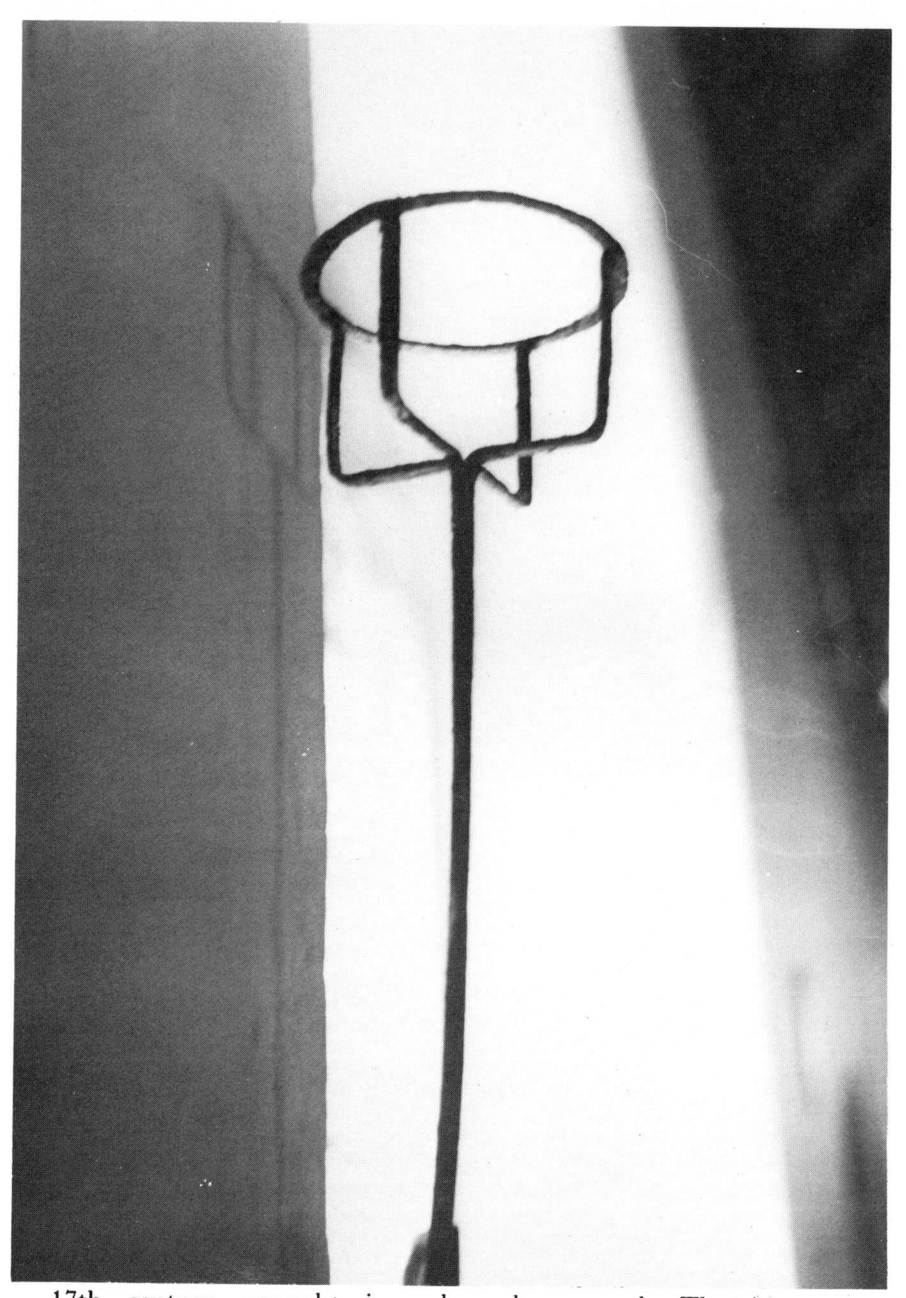

17th century wrought iron hourglass stand, Thorrington Church

One of the oldest methods of telling the time is with the aid of the hourglass and sundial, a method which can be traced back to ancient Greece and Egypt.

Many existing hourglasses are to be found in churches, housed in a wrought iron stand, close to the pulpit. The hourglass would assist the preacher to gauge the length of his sermon.

A fine, complete, 18th century example with stand executed in wrought iron and wood is in the church of St. Edmund at Abbess Roding, while at Ingatestone and Fryerning at St. Mary the Virgin and St. Edmund, a fine 11th century church, an early 18th century hourglass stand of twisted wrought iron can be seen fixed to the north wall in the nave. Another stand, this time a 17th century example also of wrought iron can be found in the nave of the parish church of All Saints, Norton Manderville, a very small parish just 2½ miles north-east of Chipping Ongar.

Mention a gate to a true-dyed-in-the-wool Essex yeoman and nine times out of ten he'll shoot you a wry grin. Through the ages the story of "Essex Calves" has followed the Essex man wherever he has gone. Many years ago a farmer's prize calf had the misfortune to jam its head between the bars of a five-bar-gate. Up rushed the locals who stood scratching their heads trying to work out a way of releasing the poor trapped animal. One bright lad, a little more astute than the others, thought of a way and soon the calf was free. He had struck off its head with an axe! Hence the nick-name "Essex Calves" which has stuck ever since.

Gates play an important part on any property, but owing to the ravages of two world wars and the urgent need for scrap iron for munitions, many fine examples have vanished into the melting pot.

One of the oldest in Essex must surely be that in Colchester known as the Balkerne Gate. Thought to be of pre-Roman origin it was first excavated during the mid-1800's, it was not until 1913–17 that the real work was carried out, much of the important research being done by the now famous Sir Mortimer Wheeler. Fenced off with iron railings, this ancient relic carries a full explanatory plaque of its history and discovery.

A fine gate of carved oak, thought to be of the 17th century, can be seen in the gardens of St. Osyth Priory, while an unusual wrought iron garden gate is to be found at Thorpe-le-Soken. This sports a Brent goose, for the owner has devoted his life to the study of this wild bird and has even turned his garden over to them. The gate to West Mersea

Wrought iron gate and home of Brent goose, Thorpe-le-Soken

yacht club has a fine wrought iron sailing ship for a motif. After all, what else would be fitting! A really superb example of early wrought iron work can be seen in the 15 ft. high double gates at Thorpe Hall, former home of the late Viscount Byng of Vimy. Lady Byng devoted much of her spare time to purchasing iron work for her lavish gardens which were rated the finest in the district. These particular gates are said to have come from a derelict mansion in Suffolk, although there is a strong legend that maintains they originated from the Embankment side of New Scotland Yard, Viscount Byng having served as Commissioner of the Metropolitan Police from 1928–31.

At Woolston Hall, Chigwell, there are a pair of early 18th century wrought iron gates with an elaborate overthrow, which are something of a local landmark.

Essex can boast more Norman doors than any other county and many still retain their original wrought iron hinges and straps, and one can note the similarity of the straps to the old medieval two-handed and hand-and-half swords. It is a fact that swordsmiths spent their slack periods forging such household metalwork.

The north door at Hadstock church is reputed to be the oldest in England, being in use when William the Conqueror invaded the country. At the church at Castle Hedingham the north and south doors bear fragments of human skin beneath the ironwork and oak. It was common practice to nail the flayed skin of a criminal to the church door as a warning to other would-be villains. At Copford, on display in the church, is an unusually well preserved piece of skin which used to be nailed to the door. It was thought to have been stripped from a captured Danish pirate.

Many strange legends exist about the doors of churches but none stranger than that of St. Mary's Church at Runwell, near Wickford. Here, on the inside of the south door is a burnt in impression of a great claw-like hand said to be the hand mark of the Devil.

Back in the ancient mists of time a local curate by the name of Rainaldus practised the Black Art within the grounds of his church. One morning whilst conducting a service with his flock Rainaldus is reported to have been confronted by the Devil who made a grab for the startled priest. Fleeing in terror the curate escaped through the south door while the Devil, unable to pass through the sanctified portals, vented his spleen by burning his mark into the old oak door. The congregation, having also escaped when the chase started, came creeping back after a suitable interval. They searched in vain for their wayward curate but all they ever found was an evil smelling puddle of

Wrought iron gates, Thorpe Hall, Thorpe

St. Mary's Church Porch, Runwell

green liquid which was bubbling away by the south porch. In the middle of this pool lay a small, flint stone resembling a human head. This was later mounted on the south wall near where Rainaldus had held the mass, and bears the Latin inscription "Stipendia peccati mors" (The wages of sin is Death).

Search around any church and you will find that the most neglected area is usually the north side, for it is here that the Prince of Darkness is said to wander around looking for lost, damned souls. It was common practice, up to a few years ago, to bury excommunicated sinners, suicides and unbaptized infants on the north side of the church.

Next time you attend a baptism service note how both south and north doors are, where possible, left open. This is so that at the words "renounce the Devil and all his works", Satan can leave unhindered through the north door.

Known as "Devil's Doors" most north doors are either blocked up with flint, rubble and mortar, or left to the elements. Just try to get to a north door without being stung or torn to pieces by nettles or wild brambles!

A selection of blocked-up north doors well worth a visit are at St. Clement's, Leigh-on-Sea; St. Nicholas, Great Wakering; All Saints, Rettendon; and St. Mary's, South Benfleet. Those unused but still intact are to be found at North Shoebury; All Saints, Barling, and the parish church at Hockley.

Lych-gates, those sombre, but at the same time finely executed pieces of craftmanship, were originally intended as a shelter for the coffin, its bearers and party of mourners. Many good examples are to be found in Essex and the oldest known ones are at Felstead and Waltham Cross. The former, a 16th century gate, has been built into the Old School House while the latter can be found at the Welsh Harp Inn. This 17th century lych-gate has also been enclosed, with a room added above. It boasts two tie-beams and wall plates with early 17th century painted inter-lacing ornament.

At Dovercourt there is a handsome lych-gate which was presented by Queen Victoria to the parish church of All Saints in 1899. In return the parish erected a suitable statue of the Queen in all her regal splendour.

Well worth searching for are the various types of weather-vane; those ornate pieces of blacksmithing art which cover a vast selection of subjects. Many strange and wonderful designs can be found and they crop up in the most unusual and out of the way places. Not all are on churches or ancient manor houses for many are to be found on farm labourers' cottages and outhouses. At Little Bentley there is a hunting scene windvane while in the Essex County Council yard at Thorring-

Medieval ironwork, Elmstead Church

Lych gate, Dovercourt

Lych gate, Thorrington

Huntsman weathervane, Little Bentley

Steam Roller weathervane, Thorrington

Sundial, High Street, Dedham

Sundial in grounds of St. Osyth Priory

Pair of scratch-dials, Elmstead Church

ton, a Steam Roller surmounts the ornate scroll work. Yet another, this time in the form of a galleon rigged out in full sail is on top of an outbuilding which used to be the stables at a house called Milldurst near Churchgate Street, Old Harlow. One of the most striking church weather vanes is that on Ugley church.

Sundials, which most people associate with garden ornaments, can be classed as one of the oldest methods of telling the time. Originally constructed from two pieces of wood and clipped together to form a "T" shape, they evolved through the ages to finally take on their now familiar shape and style.

The earliest sundials are the scratch-dials, many of which can be found on church walls, portals and buttresses. These dials were mainly used by bell-ringers to call people to mass and because of this, the line which indicates an approximation to nine o'clock, the usual hour for mass, was more emphasised than the rest. At Ashingdon St. Andrew on a buttress near the church porch, cut into the stone, is a sundial which was used by 14th century builders. Another example is to be found on a buttress by the south door at Elmstead church, while yet another which still bears traces of charcoal on the radiating line, is at St. Andrew's, Minster. The church at Chickney, has a number of scratch-dials on the south-east window of the nave and southeast window of the chancel. A square stone with incised sundial can be seen in the south wall of the chancel at Great Easton church while a most unusual glass sundial is set in the southwest window of the nave at Wenden Lofts. Other scratch-dials are to be found at Wicken Bonhunt, Lindsell, and at Clavering in the south aisle, cut in one of the south buttresses is a fragment of a sundial thought to be 18th century.

Sundials, in a form we are more used to seeing, can be found in the grounds of St. Osyth Priory and on Clacton seafront. That in the priory is of a winged man bearing a dial on his head, while the latter, set out in a well kept garden, gives directions to local towns and villages and seaward, the distances to lightships and buoys. Although this 5 ft. diameter dial is set out like a compass it is without a metal gnomon. A sign board swinging outside Dial House, Harlow, bears the date 1759 and "Waste no time" as well as a representation of a square sundial.

A rather unusual wall dial can be seen in Dedham High Street with triangular gnomon and hand-painted Roman numerals.

CHAPTER II

Gravestones, Memorials, Obelisks, Milestones, Fonts, Postboxes

Search around any graveyard in an ancient village and you will soon stumble across a tombstone or memorial tablet that carries a message which one could class as unusual or curious. In Essex these exist in great abundance so that it has been something of a problem to sift out the most colourful examples.

The most interesting gravestones were those left behind by our Roman invaders and masters, but unfortunately over the long track of time these have fallen by the wayside either being used for hardcore or the footings for some building or the other. Examples have been rescued, however, for in the Colchester Castle Museum stand several fine stones commemorating the death of legionaries.

Although not truly intended as a gravestone or come to that, a memorial, the burial mounds at Bartlow Hill, just four miles from Saffron Walden, are rated as the finest examples of Romano-British sugar-loaf burial mounds in Britain.

Travellers, finding their way along the Great Holland to Holland-on-Sea will pass, on a sharp bend, a small stone bearing the following legend, "Site of Ancient Burial Ground". When the road was being improved, between the Wars, workmen uncovered the remains of dozens of skeletons packed head to toe. It was also reported at the time that a rusty long-sword lay by the side of one skeleton. Despite numerous interviews with the remaining workmen little more has been seen or heard of this sword. The remains were identified as early Saxon.

Back once more to that ancient town of Colchester, a trip to St. Giles churchyard takes us to the black marble gravestone of two Royalist generals, Sir Charles Lucas and Sir George Lisle.

In the grim struggle that became known as the English Civil War,

Roman Legionary's tombstone, Colchester

Site of ancient burial ground, Little Holland

Essex favoured the rule of Oliver Cromwell. When Royalist troops under Lucas and Lisle stormed the walls of Colchester on June 12th 1648, the townsfolk offered little resistance knowing full well that Fairfax, the Parliamentarian leader, was only a few miles away.

Fairfax with a well trained army of between 6,000 and 7,000 men laid siege to the town and waited to starve out the Royalists who numbered just 4,000 poorly equipped men. Poorly equipped and ill-trained they may have been but the besieged garrison managed to last out for nearly three months surrendering only after all available food and ammunition had been exhausted.

It is recorded that food had become so scarce that after the horses had been eaten dogs, cats, rats and mice were scooped up for the pot. A side of a small dog changed hands for the princely sum of six shillings.

With the surrender of the Royalists a drum-head trial was held in which Lucas and Lisle were sentenced to be executed. Conducted to the north side of the castle wall the two men fell before the rough cast musket balls of the firing squad. A monument stands on the spot where legend has it grass never grows. Because it was feared that the tomb might be desecrated by irate Essex folk (the town had to raise £12,000 in fines for Fairfax), the inscription was cut extra deep into the black stone.

A man who lived under the rule of seven monarchs and Oliver Cromwell lies buried in Ramsden Bellhouse, near Billericay. Described in Mee's "Essex" as "the most remarkable child in the village", Anthony Childs died in 1726 at the grand old age of 81. He lived through the Civil War and the beheading of Charles I, through the short-lived dictatorship of Oliver Cromwell, then Charles II, James II, William and Mary, Anne, George I and George II.

One of the oldest men to have lived in Essex was William Mead, M.D., who was buried in Ware parish churchyard. He died on the 28th of October 1652 aged 148 years, 9 months, 3 weeks and 4 days. Runner-up to this title must surely be William Nicholson who lies in the neat little churchyard at Wendens Ambo, who died on December 15th 1886 aged 104. This old sea-faring man had seen service with Lord Nelson as a midshipman.

Another record must be the grave of Edward Bright, "the biggest man in England", who weighed 44 stone. His last resting place is in Maldon churchyard. When he was buried, in 1750, a special apparatus had to be fixed in the church to hold his coffin. He was a descendant of Cromwell's sister, Jane.

Links with the American Colonies have always been strong in Essex, but at Gravesend, overlooking the Thames, we find a close tie with the North American Indian. Standing in the churchyard of St. George's is the proud statue of Princess Pocahontas. The story surrounding this wild maiden is rather remarkable for after saving the life of Captain John Smith, she was educated at a missionary school and became the first North American Indian to take up Christian beliefs. Sailing to England aboard "The Treasurer", accompanied by Sir Thomas Dale, the Princess was received at the court of King James I. However, British weather being what it is she fell ill soon afterwards and died on March 21st 1617.

The tomb of Mary Ellis in the churchyard of St. Clement's, Leigh-on-Sea, deserves mention if only for the marks of latter-day vandals on the stonework. Known as the "cutlass tomb" because of the deep marks cut in the top which are thought to have been caused by members of the notorious press gangs sharpening their cutlasses as they awaited to fight off gangs of angry townsfolk trying to release "pressed" victims. Another much more reasonable theory is that the marks were nothing more sinister than the hone marks of generations of grass-cutters sharpening their scythes and bill-hooks on the handy placed stone!

Slavery, with its deep roots in Africa and America, seems a little out of place in the quiet of the Essex countryside. However, in the corner of Little Parndon churchyard lies the grave of a Negro slave, one Hester Woodley. Aged 62, she died on 13th May 1767. She had belonged to a Mrs. Bridget Woodley who on her death passed on the slave together with her other belongings to her daughter. A note of interest is the fact that she bore her mistress's surname, a common practice in the days of slavery.

Little need be said regarding the following, it speaks for itself. On the gravestone these words are scribed deep: "Martha Blewit of the Swan Inn at Bathorn-End in this Parish; buried May 7th 1681: was the Wife of nine Husbands successively, but the ninth outlived her". The Text at her Funeral Sermon was "Last of all, the Woman died also".

For those with a yen for military history the tomb lying in Weeley churchyard, of Alexander McDonald, of the Cameron Highlanders, should prove interesting.

The story takes us back to the period of the Napoleonic Wars and the year of 1806. Troops having been brought in to coastal areas to defend the Essex shore, the sleepy village of Weeley had been selected as a likely garrison. All went well until the St. James's Day Fair, held at Little Clacton, came around. All day the small, stocky, kilted

Highlanders had set the village maidens agog, and all day their swains found themselves pushed into the background as the Scots teased and tantalized the wide-eyed girls.

Things finally came to a head when a band of drunken soldiers tried to crash the village dance. After a confrontation and a wild chase near Amerell's Farm, one soldier, Alexander McDonald, having injured his leg in the fracas, got separated from his fleeing comrades. Outpacing the luckless soldier, and coming within striking distance, the irate villagers set about the hapless man, beating him to the ground with sticks and stones till he lay dead.

Although four men were eventually sent for trial at Chelmsford assize court on March 12th 1807, the evidence was so conflicting they were found not guilty.

His tomb, still tended by the Cameron Highlanders, bears the following inscription, "Under this stone lie the remains of Alexander McDonald, late soldier in the First Battalion 79th Regt., who in the prime of life was inhumanly murdered near Little Clacton on the morning of the 26th July 1806".

Another military tragedy occurred in Chelmsford when a party of German soldiers serving with the King's German Legion were burnt to death whilst sleeping in a barn behind the "Spotted Dog" Inn. The victims, numbering thirteen, were buried in the churchyard behind the Shire Hall. Another unusual grave can be found alongside the Wickford Rayleigh railway line. Cordoned off with white painted ropes and surmounted by a concrete pillar bearing an aeroplane propeller, it marks the grave of two British airmen. Taking off on the night of March 7/8th 1918 to do battle with enemy Gotha bombers, Captain H. C. Stroud, of No. 61 Squadron, Rochford, and Captain A. B.

Tomb mounted with iron spikes to ward off body snatchers, Wanstead

Kynoch, of No. 37 Squadron, Goldhanger, collided and fell to their deaths. The propeller marks the spot where the airmen fell.

On some old tombs can be found traces of iron strap work, while in Wanstead churchyard one can still see the stone watch-box. Both of these belong to the days of the "body-snatchers" or the "Resurrectionists", as they were known in higher circles. Back in the eighteenth century it was common practice for a newly buried corpse to be snatched for sale to medical students or hospitals for research. Ten to twelve guineas was the going price for a prime body and even more if it still wore its best clothes.

In 1823, Samuel Clarke of Little Leighs was convicted and sentenced to be transported for seven years, not for stealing a body, but for the theft of the clothing in which the body had been buried!

For those who could afford it an armed guard was employed to watch over the graves (hence the Wanstead watch-box), while others either bound the top of the tomb with iron straps or spent long, spooky nights standing guard over their loved ones' graves. Waiting, that is, until the body had started to decompose and was of no further use to the "Resurrectionists".

A gravestone bearing a rather odd inscription stands in St. Osyth churchyard. Although badly eroded, one can still decipher the most important part – the date.

> "Here Lieth A . . . Wife of Will R. . . .
> Who Departed This Life 17th Day of Feb.
> in ye Year 1734/5".

Gravestone, St. Osyth Churchyard . showing link with Julian Calendar of pre-1752

It appears that with the old Julian calendar of pre-1752, it was custom to count the year from March to March. It was therefore the common practice to add the next year to the tombstones of those who died in the month of February.

Closely linked with gravestones are memorials and in Essex we have many to choose from. At North Weald Basset we find "Basset's Pole" named after Ralph Basset, son of the Lord Chief Justice to Henry III, as a memorial after he had been killed in battle at Eversham in 1265.

At Spains Hall, Finchingfield, is a plaque commemorating the foundation of the Borstal Institute by Sir Evelyn John Ruggles-Brise, K.C.B.

In this day and age of speeding coaches, buses and trains one gives little thought as to how it all started. The next time you queue for a bus spare a thought for George Shillibeer, inventor of the London omnibus back in July 1829. Plying between the Yorkshire Stingo brewery in Marylebone Road and the City, for the fare of one shilling, his bus was drawn by three horses. Stage coaches charged 2/6d. for the same journey. His memorial tablet can be seen in Chigwell parish church, erected by London busmen to perpetuate his memory.

A rather unusual memorial can be found in Ugley Church. Painted on a board it reads: "Benefactor Mr. Robt. Bucke, Draper, Born at Ugley in Essex, by his Will dated 27th day of Nov. 1620. Gave 3 Suits of clothes to 3 poor Men and 3 suits to 3 poor Women with Hats, and 3 pounds in Money, for makeing Ditto. to be given at the Discretion of the Church-Wardens at Ugley every 3rd Year for Ever. The Land tied for the Performance hereof Lieth at CARRING in KENT."

War memorials are most poignant especially when the victim or victims were either women or non-combatants. One of the most well-known World War I heroines was Nurse Cavell, who was shot by the Germans on October 12th 1915, for helping Belgian, French and British soldiers to escape. A memorial to her can be found in the Church of Steeple Bumpstead.

Three memorials to one man must surely be something of a record, but to the gallant Captain Fryatt goes just that honour. At Dovercourt one finds a memorial stone to this sailor, who aboard his ship the "Brussels" was instrumental in ramming a German U-Boat in 1915. He was later captured and shot. The flag-staff of his ship is to be found at Wadham Lodge sports ground, Walthamstow, together with a notice of his deeds. Another memorial to do with this man, although not in Essex, is to be found on Mount Fryatt in Alberta, Canada.

Memorials to the enemy dead exist extensively on the Essex coast, but one of the most outstanding is that in Great Burstead churchyard

Memorial to Captain Fryatt

where headstones to the crew of the Zeppelin L 32 can be found. Shot down in flames on September 24th 1916 at 12.45 a.m., twenty-two men met their end in a most terrible manner.

Another Zeppelin which suffered considerable damage from British guns and was forced to land at Little Wigborough was the L 33.

No one was injured as the pilot settled the airship across the little country lane. Forming up his crew, he fired a Very flare into the side of the airship, turning the 600 ft. long monster into a blazing inferno. Setting off towards the coast road Captain Böcker and his crew attempted to make good their escape, but after marching only a few hundred yards they were captured by a patrolling policeman.

The remains of the L 33 lay on show for a considerable time before being cut up for the scrapyard. Little is left now of the aerial dinosaur, but a visit to Great Wigborough church reveals a frame made-up from fragments of the wreckage, containing the story of the incident, while in the tower one can see part of the aluminium fuselage.

The wrath of the sea has always been something to reckon with and in the church at Brightlingsea a rather unique row of memorial tablets to seamen is set in the wall. During the late 19th century the vicar, the Rev. Arthur Pertwee, used to be seen, in stormy weather, standing aloft in his church tower with lantern in hand guiding home local fishermen to safety. Later he hit upon the idea of the wall-memorials to commemorate the loss of Brightlingsea sailormen.

Also at Brightlingsea church is the Nicholas Magens memorial designed by N. Read in 1779. This is a truly opulent piece of work and one well worth seeing. Visitors from America may smile to themselves

Memorial Tablets, Brightlingsea Church

Nicholas Magens memorial designed by N. Read 1779

and with good reason, as California is shown on the globe as being a small island!

No list of Essex memorials is complete without mention of the Battles of Hastings and Waterloo.

At North Benfleet church a memorial tablet stands to John Cole, a soldier at Waterloo. At the celebrated command "Up Guards, and at 'em", he was wounded by a musket ball, but fought on until the victory. He died in Benfleet on April 10th, 1836 aged 51, bequesting his medal to the curate, whose last act was the erection of this tablet.

The date 1066 must be the only date that most people remember alongside their own birthday. At Waltham Abbey is a stone marking the position of the former high altar behind which King Harold is said to have been buried after the battle of Hastings. One of the strangest memorials must be that sitting in Dedham parish churchyard against the south wall of the church. Here, a large boulder some three feet high carries the name of Edward and Martha Ward. A story, written in 1907, reports that Edward Ward, a ploughman, was turning a field one day, when the share of his plough struck hard against a large object. Finding it to be a huge boulder he hit upon the novel idea of having it for his tombstone. It is thought to be a spent thunderbolt.

Essex has always been famous for its martyrs be they industrial or religious and during the reign of Queen Mary, 1553–8, a wholesale persecution of Protestants throughout England was undertaken. Over 300 people were burnt in Mary's reign, and of this number at least 72 suffered in Essex, chiefly at Colchester, Stratford, and Brentwood. In 1555, the persecution was raging fiercely in Colchester, for no less than 22 people of that town were dragged through the streets of London on their way to trial; and during the next three years about 22 persons, both men and women, were burnt at Colchester. A monument to the memory of these martyrs was erected in 1843 and can be seen in the Town Hall carrying this inscription:

"In memory of Those Blessed Martyrs for Christ,
who during the reign of Queen Mary,
WERE BURNT ALIVE IN THIS TOWN OF COLCHESTER, FOR THEIR FIRM ADHERENCE TO THE PROTESTANT FAITH."

Obelisks figure prominently in Essex and whilst on the subject of martyrs the granite example situated just outside Brentwood marks the spot where 19-year-old William Hunter paid the supreme penalty for his religious beliefs.

"To the Pious Memory of William Hunter,
A Native of Brentwood,

Who was Condemned, at the early age of 19, by
Bishop Bonner, in the Reign of Queen Mary,
and Burnt at the Stake near this spot,
MARCH XXVI, MDLV.

Another obelisk with an interesting history is to be found in a field adjoining The Warren, Loughton. It is said to be a memorial to a horse ridden at Waterloo by General Grosvenor, close friend of the Duke of Wellington.

Not an obelisk but a seventy foot high stone column in Colne Park close to Colne Engaine, is the memorial built in 1791 by the well known architect J. Soane, who also designed the Bank of England. This boasts a handsome copper urn on the upperwork. On one of the blocks of stone at the base of the monument is the following inscription:

MICHAEL ROBERTO HILLS arn PHILIPPUS HILLS
observantae ergo p. MDCCLXXXXI.

A strange and somewhat amusing story is told by the locals about this monument. During the Second World War American servicemen infested the public houses for miles around. A kind of feud existed between these GI's and the locals as the former bent the ear of all and sundry with stories both tall and wild about the USA. One evening, an American serviceman enquired what was in the copper urn set way up on top of the column. A local told him, with tongue in cheek, that "it be filled with liquid gold, that's for sure!"

Nothing else was said, but a couple of nights later the sound of machine-gun fire was heard. Later, it was discovered that the copper urn was riddled with bullet holes, some twenty-eight to thirty holes which can still be seen to this day!

The earliest known form of milestone are those called "Pudding-stones" known to geologists as conglomerates. These large boulders resemble the old fashioned plum-pudding, the fruit being flint pebbles in a silica matrix. The average size is something like three feet in height and about eighty inches around the base.

A track of these boulders stretches like a row of ancient markers across the county and can be found in Norfolk, Suffolk, Buckinghamshire, Oxfordshire and far beyond. In Essex, a line stretches from the River Lea towards Epping Upland, Marks Tey, in the churchyard of Beauchamp Roding, at Holyfield, a small hamlet near Waltham Abbey, White Notley, Mashbury, and Ugley Green next to the village pump.

They are believed to date back to 5,000 B.C., and there is a school of thought that reckons the stones were used as milestones by nomadic tribes of Ancient Britain. A number have in fact been built into church

Pudding stone, Forge Cottage, White Notley

walls and foundations as can be seen in the north wall of Magdalen Laver Church and the south wall of Broomfield church, near Chelmsford.

Although not strictly classed as milestones, although they did in fact double as such, are boulders. At Newport, adjoining the site of a leper hospital is a giant glacial boulder on which in bygone days, medieval travellers would place alms for the lepers. On the roadside at Arkenden is a large stone known locally as the "Sarsen Stone" dragged to its resting place by neolithic people for use as a chamber tomb but later utilized as a marker or milestone. A milestone with a difference is that situated on One Tree Hill at Langdon Hill, Basildon. Of some four feet in height, the top of this carries an indicator showing various landmarks for miles around. It is also used as a triangulation point by the Ordnance Survey.

At Loughton, we find a fine example of an 18th century milestone. Situated at the top of Golding's Hill, this old and worn stone carries the wording, "Loughton parish. Epping 3. London 13." It was erected by the Epping and Ongar Highway Trust which was set up by an Act of 1787 to maintain the road from Woodford to Harlow.

Other milestones can be found at Wrabness, Mistley, and on the B1352 road from Ramsey to Manningtree.

Most churches are equipped with a font and in Essex they range in all shapes and sizes. The oldest font in Essex is the rudely ornamented bowl standing in the church at Little Maplestead, which is thought to be 11th century. At Pentlow and Belchamp Walter are 12th century fonts, the one at Pentlow being richly but crudely carved. A good selection of 15th century fonts can be found in Essex and those of outstanding workmanship can be found at Halstead, Chickney, Bulmer and Gestingthorpe. Fonts that are enclosed with rich and ornate cases of panelling which terminate in gabled and pinnacled spires of the early 16th century period can be seen at Littlebury, Thaxted, and Pentlow.

A most unusual font constructed entirely of oak can be found at Marks Tey with a cover made in the style of the 17th century, while at Tollesbury a font donated by John Norman, who had been found guilty of talking and swearing during the service, bears the following inscription,

> "Good people all, I pray, take care.
> That in ye church you do not swear
> as this man did."

Rather than be prosecuted he paid £5 for the font, having it thus inscribed.

A font having one of the most ornate and tallest font covers in Essex is at Takeley, while a good runner-up must surely be the 16th century example at Thaxted.

An everyday object so much taken for granted is the familiar red pillar post box. When next out for a stroll make a note of the different cyphers that stand proud on the heavily painted, weather-beaten door. They were first introduced about 1861, although in the Post Office archives there is a sketch executed in August 1857 of a proto-type wall posting box. Twenty-five at 2 guineas each were at first ordered to be tried out at various villages by the Post Office officials. In 1862, owing to complaints by house-holders who objected to the bulkiness of the large box, a smaller version was made. Not until 1871 did the boxes carry an enamel notice giving the times of collections.

Essex can lay claim to being one of the earliest counties to have wall boxes erected and between the years 1860 and 1866 places as far apart as Colchester, Leytonstone, Bow, Waltham Abbey, Grays Thurrock, Walthamstow, Romford and Chigwell all became proud possessors of

Gables and pinnacled spires of 16th century font, Thaxted

Victorian wall box, Thorpe-le-Soken

Edward VIII postbox, Colchester

the familiar red box.

An early Victorian small wall box can be seen at the Cattle Market, Colchester, while at Dedham Post Office one can see a "Ludlow" Victorian box. This is an iron box mounted in a wooden framework.

At Brightlingsea there is a Victorian round pillar box and another in Magdalen Street, Colchester. Edward VII pillar boxes are somewhat distinctive with the cypher picked out in a series of dots. These are fairly thin upon the ground, for this monarch only reigned from 1902–10. Boxes bearing his cypher are to be found at Layer-de-la-Haye and at Wellesley Road, Clacton-on-Sea.

Rarest of all post boxes must be those of Edward VIII, the king who was forced to abdicate in 1936. Examples of these can be found on the corner of Studley Drive and Wanstead Park Road, Ilford, and Glen Avenue, Colchester.

CHAPTER III

Castles, Forts, Martello Towers, Cannon, Follies

Castles, forts, and towers no matter what size or condition they may be in, always seem to re-awaken childhood dreams of knights in shining armour, dragons, long-nailed witches and things that go bump in the night. Essex has its fair share of ancient defences although many have suffered from the onslaught of vandals and redevelopment.

Colchester, one of the oldest known towns in Britain boasts a fine Norman Castle. Built on the remains of a Roman temple said to have been razed to the ground by a rampaging Boadicea, this Norman fortification consisted of an inner bailey, with the Keep or Great Tower in the middle and an outer bailey covering the ground between the inner bailey and the north wall of the town.

The Keep or Great Tower was built and the earthworks raised during the late 11th century. It can be classed as the most important remains of medieval military architecture. In area it is the largest Norman Keep now remaining in the country, being twice the size of

Remains of Norman castle, Colchester

the White Tower of London. Originally of three or more storeys it is now of just two storeys with substructures. The walls, 15ft. thick in parts, are built of coursed rubble, consisting of septaria, Roman brick, and ragstone, with dressings of Roman brick, Barnack, Caen and other freestones. A wide staircase leads to the main floor and to the top of the walls, along which it is possible to walk. The largest chamber now houses the museum, where may be seen many Roman remains which have been found in Essex. It is thought that this famous castle was built in 1078, by Eudo Dopifer, who was High Steward to William. On the ground floor is a dungeon, and at one of the angles of the Keep is a remarkable turret or watch-tower with a unique domed roof.

Up to the north of Essex we find the remains of Castle Hedingham, stronghold of the De Veres, Earls of Oxford. The Keep was built about 1130-40 but late in the 15th or early 16th century most of the original buildings were rebuilt including the Bridge, Curtain, Great Hall and various towers. Three towers are said to have been destoyed late in the 16th century. The castle, built on the summit of a steep hill, is 100 feet high and constructed from flint and rubble-stone, with walls 12 feet thick. Although razed about 800 years ago considerable damage to outbuildings occurred during the 17th and 18th centuries.

A castle with a difference which must surely be classed as a true curiosity is that to be found in the garden of a house belonging to Mr F. Littlewood at Ramsey, a village between Harwich and Manningtree.

Castle in a garden, Ramsey

Built over a period of years this fairyland castle is made from all manner of odd shaped rocks, pieces of glass, pipes and bottles. Many of the more intricate figures that lurk in the numerous nooks and crannies are hand carved taking the form of princesses, imps and dragons.

Castles are rather thin upon the ground in Essex but one that can be linked with murder and intrigue is Hadleigh Castle. Now preserved as an ancient monument by the Department of the Environment, this crumbling ruin can trace its history back to the year 1231. Started by the then Lord Chief Justice of England, Hubert de Burgh, as a defence against marauding pirates it saw very little action, but served as a popular hunting lodge and summer residence for members of the court. Among the many distinguished visitors was the Duke of Gloucester, uncle to Richard II, who rested at the Castle overnight before being ambushed and murdered on his way to London. About 1553 it was sold and demolition started but owing to a change of plans the project was abandoned leaving it in its present ruinous condition.

At Saffron Walden we find remains of a Norman watchtower or fortress. Originally a massive Keep of about forty feet square with walls 13 to 14 feet thick it was built of flint rubble cemented with lime. During the Napoleonic Wars it was used as an emergency signal station by local militia.

A fort which still retains a magnificent gatehouse is the Tilbury Fort to be found on the south Essex coast. Built as a blockhouse during the reign of Henry VIII it was later modified and strengthened to meet the threat of the Spanish Armada in 1588. Later, after the successful attack by the Dutch during the 1660's, in which they pillaged Canvey Island, exchanged shots with Harwich and proceeded to the Royal dockyards where they damaged the "Royal Oak" and the "Royal James", while the newly built "Loyal London" was reduced to ashes. King Charles had his Chief Engineer, Sir Bernard de Gomme, rebuild and design the fort. So impressive a bastion was the finished work that Daniel Defoe observed "they must be bold fellows who will venture in the biggest ships the world has ever heard of to pass such a battery". This was a case of shutting the stable door after the horse had bolted, for not only had the Dutch tweaked the royal nose by damaging His Majesty's Royal Navy but adding insult to injury, the Dutch Admiral Michiel De Ruyter, commander of the raiding squadron had seized the magnificent 96 gun battleship Royal Charles and converted it into his flagship.

Tilbury Fort is on record as being "The best preserved and in many ways the finest surviving example of late seventeenth century military engineering in England". Set out in a pentagon, with bastions, barracks, subterranian magazines, and a water-gate, this impressive piece of military architecture was never called upon to resist enemy invasion, only serving as a depot and recruiting base.

After the battle of Culloden, in 1746 Scottish survivors captured alive were given a quick "drum-head" trial and shipped off to Tilbury to await transportion to the colonies. Many men died in the terrible cramped, insanitary conditions with 300 or more crammed down in the fort's powder magazine. Trips were organised and folk came from miles around to view the wild Highlanders caged like so many animals in the stinking holds.

A landmark which is a dominant feature of the Walton-on-Naze coast is the eighty feet tower perched on the cliff top at the Naze. Built by Trinity House in 1796 as a landmark and beacon for shipping entering Harwich harbour this impressive polygonal building is of seven storeys with enbattled top. During World War II the tower carried a radar aerial and was a well known landmark for both allied and enemy aircraft. It is still used by Trinity House as a navigational aid for shipping and during the local carnival week doubles as a launching platform for the clay-pigeon shoot.

Stretching around the south-east coast one can see the remains of a battery of squat, strongly built towers, most of which are in various stages of disrepair. These are the famous Martello Towers erected during the Napoleonic Wars as a defence against the threatened invasion. Eleven Martello Towers were erected in Essex, at a cost of some £225,000. Styled on a fortress which the British had tried to storm off the coast of Sicily during the late 18th century, a whole network of these towers was planned and built. Each tower was round in shape, 140 feet in circumference, 32 feet high and with walls from eight to twelve feet thick. Quarters were built within to house officers and men, also a kitchen and a deep well, capable of supplying the garrison in case of a lengthy siege. In some a battery was built on the foreshore in front of the towers. These batteries, comprised of a low brick platform, supported five iron 24-pounder cannon, a magazine with walls five feet thick, and a guardroom. The one chosen mainly for its general state of preservation and availability is Tower "D" situated on a stretch of foreshore which used to be called Eastness between Jaywick and Clacton and adjacent to the golf course. This particular tower was built around 1809 and designed to hold approximately 24 men.

The battery, which up to the 1930's could be seen lying some 150 yards in front of the tower has already been demolished by the

18th century tower built by Trinity House, Walton-on-Naze

Martello Tower, Clacton

encroaching sea, its five cannon swallowed up by the shifting sand and grey mud. Visitors to the spot, if lucky enough to choose an ebb tide, can still find remains of the brick foundations and platform, while for those with a keen eye a close search among the small waterfilled hollows in the mud could find a spent musket or pistol ball.

Each tower was supplied with a long 24-pounder mounted on a bomb-proof rampart, supplemented in certain other towers with two short 24-pounders. The remainder boasted a 5½ inch howitzer.

The method of loading each piece was a highly complicated and sometimes dangerous business. One method was to have the gunpowder packed ready in cotton bags. Breaking the bag took only a second aided with a sharp spike via the touch-hole. Sprinkling priming powder around the hole and pan surrounding it, the gunner made ready with a smouldering match, or red hot iron.

Although the towers were manned from time to time they were never garrisoned in anger. The soldiers who waited ready to man Tower "D" were stationed at Weeley Barracks and they had to make the long, hot, two hour trek to take up battle stations when the signal beacons were lit to hail impending invasion. When the Napoleonic wars were over the towers were used to house retired coastguard and naval personnel and their families, but owing to the damp and bleak windswept conditions they were soon abandoned, falling into disrepair. During World War II the towers served once again as look-out posts but the antiquated weapons were scrapped and unfortunately lost for all time.

Tower "D" is now vacant, having been abandoned by the Civil Defence Corps. It can only be a matter of a few decades before this too suffers the same fate as its battery. Tower "F" on the Marine Parade surrounded by an impressive 37 ft. wide moat still serves as a coast-guard observation post while local Sea Cadets use the inner depths as their headquarters and training centre. Others exist at Point Clear, Walton-on-Naze, Jaywick and Clacton.

A fortification which can lay claim to being one of the best preserved examples of early 19th century military architecture is the Redoubt at Harwich. Built between 1808 and 1810 during the Napoleonic Wars using French prisoners of war for labourers, this mammoth circular fortification is about 200 ft. in diameter with a central courtyard of some 85 ft. in diameter. The walls are 8 ft. thick of hard baked brick, set in Roman cement, excavated from the Beacon Cliff, Harwich. The only approach is over a drawbridge across a 20 ft. deep dry moat.

The Redoubt was originally armed with ten 24 pounder cannon but later in 1861-2 these were replaced by a selection of twelve ton, R.M.L. Mark V muzzle-loader cannon, one of which has been excavated and put on display in the Redoubt. Originally the fortress was intended to hold some 300 men and in effect was self supporting with a well and cooking area. This deep well is still to be seen in the courtyard. Built in two levels most of the eighteen rooms carry historical names such as "Pepys" (M.P. for Harwich and Secretary to the Navy during the 17th-century), "Jones", (Captain of the Mayflower who lived in King's Head Street during the 16th/17th centuries), and "De Vere", (first Lord of the Manor who lived at Castle Hedingham during the 11th century). Others have local connections with families who have served Harwich for centuries.

Now classified as an ancient monument the Redoubt is being restored by members of the Harwich Society, Redoubt Action Group. Many items of interest have been sifted from the silt, among them a selection of regimental army buttons, dominoes made out of sea-shells and the remains of a few clay pipes.

Closely linked with these fortifications is the odd cannon scattered around the county. In the Harwich Redoubt there is a badly corroded example mounted in the "Pepys" room which had been recovered from a nearby beach. It is thought to be from a 17th century Swedish naval ship. Another Redoubt cannon is embedded in the concrete at Cook Street, Harwich.

Cannon at Martello Tower, Jaywick

On the site of the old Warley Barracks, Brentwood, we find a 28 pounder cannon with a ball sealed in the muzzle and its breech embedded into the ground. This was one of the original guns brought back by the Essex Regiment from India. It served with the old East India Company and saw action during the Indian Mutiny of 1857. Another, this time with a "Charge of the Light Brigade" flavour is the well preserved cannon mounted on its original cast-iron carriage in the grounds of Chelmsford Museum, (Oaklands House). It saw service during the battle of Sebastopol in 1855 being brought back and presented to the town by Major S. J. Skinner in 1858. At Point Clear, by the side of the Martello Tower is a 24-pounder embedded breech-end first and serving as an unusual bird-bath and table.

Whilst searching for castles and forts one is likely to stumble across a folly or two. In Essex, follies as such, seem to be in short supply but a rather odd creation is to be found at Pentlow. Dubbed Bull's Tower this odd shaped building was built by Edward Bull in memory of his father. It is thought to be late 19th century. A folly with a medieval overtone is to be found in the garden of the Minories, Colchester. Known as the "Gothic Summer House", it was added to over the years and a fair amount of Roman rubble was utilised. Mention of this folly is made in Morant's mammoth work dated 1741. Still in Colchester is a mid 18th century folly built on the remains of an old dovecote building to be seen by the goldfish pond in the Castle grounds. This was built by Charles Gray who was responsible for extensive development in the area during that period.

Although of no great age the embattled Keep and chimneys of the Warwick Castle, Clacton, dominate the centre of the town. Built during the latter part of the 19th century it was planned and built by W. J. Hook Esq. as a form of grandiose hotel, along the style of an ancient castle. Over the years its out-buildings have been demolished until today it stands as a rather tired and neglected public house with the wild elements taking their annual toll of its structure.

The Warwick Castle, 19th century folly, Clacton

CHAPTER IV

Windmills, Treadmills, Thatch and Thatchers, Mounting Blocks & Steps

When one talks of windmills one has an immediate association with Holland with its dykes, clogs and be-frocked rosy cheeked maidens. Very little thought is given to the windmills and postmills that remain scattered around our own county, some in a good state of repair while others stand in skeletal disrepair with paint and timbers peeling, ravaged and beaten by the elements, and a home for countless number of vermin.

Up to 1965 there were 28 windmills in Essex ranging from post, tower, smock and composite mills. Not all were in working order, for many were nothing more than derelict wrecks which since that time have been demolished.

A number of preservation societies have worked hard to rebuild those mills worth saving and a few have now been preserved as buildings of historical interest, choice examples being the Thaxted mill originally built by a John Webb in 1804, and the tower variety at Stock, now owned by the County Council and maintained by them as an ancient monument. The restored tower mill at Stansted and the postmill at Bocking are well worth visiting, the latter having a collection of restored farm implements on display. One of the finest examples of tower mills is that at Great Bardfield known as the Gibraltar Mill. It is thought to be originally an Elizabethan mill which was converted in 1749 for use as a cottage, later to be converted in 1751 back to a windmill.

Windmills have been part of the Essex scene for hundreds of years and in fact a "common sail" can be seen in a stained glass window, known to be circa 1500, in the north aisle of the church at Clavering.

The three main types of windmill are the post, tower and smock

Postmill, Finchingfield

Remains of Towermill, Tiptree

mills, while the composite mill was usually constructed from old post mills having the post removed and the body mounted on wheels or castors which in turn ran on a track surmounted on the walls of a roundhouse.

The postmill, a well built wood framed building, was mounted on a well seasoned, upright post, usually of pitch pine, oak, elm, or in the case of Morteton mill, sycamore, which in turn was slung on top of a brick built, tarred, round house. Early postmills were much lower and smaller, being pushed round into the wind by aid of a long tail pole. They had to be that much lower to the ground because the sail cloth which was stretched over the open framework of the sail could only be fitted and adjusted from the ground level. Later, with the advent of the patent shutter and draw-string the body was built taller and sails extended longer. Most mills were equipped with four sails although examples of five, six and eight-sailers have been known. The patent sail saw the introduction of extra long sails with a span from fifty-five to eighty feet, the long "whips" usually built from seasoned lengths of pitch pine. The cloth was held in place by a series of rings and eyelets and by means of a selection of cords called pointing lines, could be adjusted according to the strength of the wind. With these pointing lines it was possible to give four settings to the sails; sword point, dagger point, full sail and first reef.

There was an art in operating a windmill, for not only had the miller to possess a full working knowledge of his mill but he had to be fairly conversant with the local weather conditions. Many contemporary reports give colourful accounts of windmills having fan-tails, sails and even the complete cap blown off to be tossed like so much tumble-weed across the meadows in a gale-force wind. All because the miller was not to hand or if he was, because he could not turn his mill out of the direct force of the storm. The most important items on a mill were the two wind indicators which were designed to tell the miller just when to move his charge. If both fans revolved the mill was true enough into the wind for it to operate efficiently, but if one stopped he then knew it was time to turn the mill.

The postmill varied very little in construction from country to country, for even in France and Holland the substructure of the mill is based on three crosstrees and six quartern bars which gave added stability. Each post had a steady bearing at the main point where it passed through the bottom floor of the body formed by two thick legs or sheers on either side of it.

Towermills were in the main usually round, but a fine early 18th century red brick mill known as the Gibraltar Mill, at Great Bardfield, proves the exception for this tower is octagonal leading to sixteen sides then a rounded top section. Being brick built it would seem, on the face of it, to be much stronger and less vulnerable than the timber post and smock mills. However, on some of these brick built towers it was often found that they did have a tendency to sink on one side, usually under the weight of the straining sail. It was fairly common practice for a millwright to jackup and underpin the sinking tower brickwork. Cracks also appeared in the side of the tower mainly for the same reason, although a chief fault lay with the builder who would insist in arranging the windows one above the other instead of staggering them around the tower. It became common practice to girth the tower with iron bands in several places. One Essex mill to receive such treatment was the Stansted mill.

Smock mills, which derive the name from their white painted walls resembling a miller's smock, are usually octagonal, although examples did exist of ten or twelve-sided mills. They have a tapered timber frame usually mounted on a brick base which sometimes incorporated a basement. This base could vary from a few feet to several storeys, but it is common, while demolishing derelict mills, to find the remains of old mill stones serving as foundation stones. This supports the theory of many historians that it was common practice to erect new mills on the site of former ones. Some post and smock mills have been known to be re-sited and on such occasions it was usual to declare a family outing and holiday to watch the great move when the tall, white painted tower, mounted on the backs of several horse-drawn carts, would slowly glide down the winding country lanes to take up a fresh position. Such must have been the excitement and holiday spirit that prevailed when the windmill at Cressing, built in 1770, was moved to Terling in 1830. This rather famous mill co-starred with the late Will Hay in his film "Oh, Mr. Porter!". This old mill is one of the last surviving smock mills in Essex, and was in use until 1950. At one time, together with other mills in Essex, it was painted white but with the advent of Zeppelin airships during World War I and the general air raid scare, it became Government policy to either demolish the mills or, as in the case of the Terling mill, to paint them all black.

One of the most important parts of a tower or smock mill is the cap which carries the sails and houses the driving shaft. It is here that the full power of the wind is transmitted down to the spinning stones. These caps came in all shapes and sizes and are called by a selection of colourful names; ogee, dome, boat or pepperpot. Some were surmounted by an ornate acorn or ball finial while others were painted in broad red, white and blue stripes. Lightning, always a danger to such high-riding structures, would often strike these finials splitting them from top to bottom.

This cap, sometimes erroneously referred to as a cupola, resembled an upturned boat, and in fact its construction was very similar to a heavyweight dingy. The construction consisted of a horizontal framework on which were fixed the rafters over which roof covering was fastened. This in turn was covered in linen which was then painted with several coats of white lead. Once in place the cap could manoeuvre itself into the wind with the aid of the sails and tail-vane, running around the top of the track on a series of iron or wooden wheels and in some instances, giant ball-bearings. Shrinkage and wear and tear were the main dangers, for if the cap jammed the works would grind to a halt. Bearings, usually constructed from a hardwood such as elm, oak, and lignum vitae were later, as methods improved, replaced by hard brass or gun metal. It was not uncommon for the millwright to melt down old brass candlesticks, horse brasses, handbells, and pestle mortars to cast a set of suitable bearings for the mill. A great fire risk was always on hand when the mill was under full power, for if the bearings did not receive their liberal ration of axle grease they would soon run dry and start to burn.

The granite stones which grind the corn measure between 2–4 feet in diameter and were re-enforced with an iron band or rim known as a mill rind. This protected the edges of the stone and prevented cracking or fracture when under full power.

Back in the early days the mill stones came from local sources but as ideas progressed they were replaced with such stones as Cullen or blue, a German lava; French or burr, a freshwater quartz; and Peak or grey, a millstone grit. The German lava stone was used mainly for grinding oats or barley, while burr was used for fine flour. The Peak or grey being only fit for animal feed. Although some of these old stones were in use up to World War I, it became normal to work a stone usually made from a composite mixture such as emery.

The mill stones, which really took a beating, could work between dressings for about 10 to 14 days but after this period has to be dressed. This work could be carried out by the miller himself or by a stone dresser. Whoever did the job however, had to exercise great care in separating the heavy stones. Special tools were used to dress a mill stone such as steel picks and bills, both double edged, and wedged into heads of wooden holders known as thrifts. These, together with a mahogany staff, a set of furrowing strips, a tin of raddle and a selection of wooden wedges make up the kit of a stone dresser who just like his forerunner, the itinerant knife-grinder or tinker, would make his way from mill to mill offering his specialised services. Like the flint-knappers of Brandon, Suffolk, who still operate today, a stone-dresser could always be recognised by the small blue scars to hands and face, caused by steel splinters from picks and bills spinning off the granite to find a soft billet.

The workings of a mill were really advanced for the times for over the years the miller and millwright between them perfected all manner of gadgets to speed up production and save labour. One of these was a warning bell which told the miller when the sacks were filled with flour, while at the same time cut off the supply of grain.

Closely associated with the tall, wind-swept windmills are the old watermills that rely solely on the rolling stream to furnish the power to turn their stones. A smock mill, at South Ockendon, built on the edge of a mill pond, once sported a water-wheel which drove a pair of extra stones down in the cellar. Another interesting watermill is Strait's Mill, Braintree. A windmill was also used to draw water at Harwich during the latter part of the 18th century for in "An Account of the Commencement and Progress of Sinking Wells at Sheerness, Harwich and Languard Fort" we read, "The machinery of the well is made to draw water by wind or horses, in calm weather by the latter, and never to have the two powers of wind and horses used at the same time. The operation should be under the care of a skilful man, to reside on the spot."

A rather unique treadmill can be seen at Berden, north of Bishops Stortford. With a twenty foot high oak wheel it can draw up and lower two eighteen gallon buckets by means of a giant cog. Wheel, cog, struts, buckets and wheel-house are all of oak and there is only one other treadmill like it in Britain, that being on the Isle of Wight.

Although not directly associated with windmills, the age old art of thatching does have an indirect link through the straw they both used. Whereas the miller would reduce the straw to chaff the thatcher would try to find the longest he could.

Thatching is one of the oldest crafts known to man and in England we find reference to it as far back as 702 A.D. There are three types of thatch in Essex today; long straw, combed wheat reed, and Norfolk water reed. Norfolk reeding is the most durable of all thatching materials, which is one good reason why the present trend is towards this type of thatching. Nowadays, with modern methods of harvesting which shreds the straw, reeds have to be grown especially for the thatchers. These are gathered in vast quantities in the Norfolk marshes, starting in December and finishing in late April. If Norfolk water reed is unobtainable then a very popular second is rye or wheat straw. The style of thatch differs from county to county but Essex still retains a close link with the Dutch settlers who built their famous round houses during the 14th and 15th centuries on the Essex coast. Canvey Island boasts a fine pair of these round houses, which were built by Dutch engineers in the year 1622 when they turned the original six small islands into the Canvey Island we know so well today.

A rather unusual example of thatch can be found at Stebbing Green, where a thatched railway coach bearing the rather distinct name of "Hill View" can be seen. Originally purchased from the L.N.E.R. at Stratford during the early 1920's the owner had it thatched in its present attractive manner. Two churches which boast thatched roofs are the Anglican, St. Francis, at Silver End and the small hamlet church at Duddenhoe End, near Saffron Walden.

Searching around the countryside will reveal all manner of different patterns, shapes and designs in the thatch, in fact after a little practice it is possible to spot the works of different craftsmen, some buildings being as far apart as 100 to 200 miles, and both thatched by the same man.

For those who reckon that thatching is a dying craft it would be truer to say that it is the craftsmen who are dying and not the craft. Out of the 200 thatchers in England 50 live and work from Essex. It takes one month to complete a job (providing the sunny weather holds out!), and whereas seventy years ago a cottage could be thatched for between £20–£30, today, the same job will cost somewhere around £400 to £500. Insurance is very high although it is common today to dip the straw in a fireproof solution before starting the operation. Even so, it is still a wise precaution to sport a fire-hook, a long handled tool often seen mounted beside a thatched building, in case of fire. Thus, if quick off the mark, it is possible to rake off the top layer of burning straw before it takes too firm a hold. A fine example of a fire-hook can be seen outside the Guildhall in Thaxted.

It is not only cottages, barns and houses that have to be thatched, for around Essex one can often find small, private wells and gate-houses topped with an ornate thatching. With a season strictly limited by the weather – in winter loss of work being something like 8–10 weeks – the thatcher finds his working day during the summer months literally stretches from dawn to dusk. It takes five years to thoroughly train a lad who, working with tools that have changed very little over the centuries, will cut and shape the straw into all manner of rustic patterns and designs. The number of tools will vary from district to district but basically they consist of a bill-hook, paring knife and a

15th century Dutch "round-house"

Thatched dis-used railway carriage, Stebbing

forked stick. Tarred twine and a collection of wooden pegs of hazel or willow complete the thatcher's equipment.

Straw also has other uses apart from that of thatching as can be witnessed in the church of St. Peter and St. Paul at Little Saling where there are four panels of straw weaving in the form of vines laden with grapes, and two panels of stars and crosses. It is thought they date back to the year 1880.

The art of straw weaving can be traced back into the dark days of history, for up to World War I it was looked upon with awe by countryfolk. Even today, in the remote parts of Essex and Suffolk the presence of a straw dolly, twisted into a certain shape, can set the tongues a-wagging, for these ancient links with fertility and witchcraft rites, twisted into all manner of strange shapes and designs, still mean a lot to the country people. In Essex, the heart of the corn dolly industry must surely be at Great Bardfield where the greatest collection of dollies is on show in the Bardfield Cottage Museum, open Saturdays and Sundays from 2 p.m., April to October. Also on display is a fine collection of small farm tools and implements.

Links with the old horse age are still to be found in Essex although many are now showing signs of wear and tear. When visiting picturesque Bradwell note the old mounting block, its five weather-beaten steps worn and twisted by countless numbers of feet as riders drew their horses alongside the granite blocks before mounting up. Another creaking example can be found outside the church at Epping Upland, while a unique set of steps which must be classed as the oddest steps in Essex must surely be those situated outside the grand old Gibraltar Mill at Great Bardfield. These are made from several old mill stones and wooden gear wheels dating back nearly 200 years.

With the ever increasing likelihood of an energy crisis and the demise of the motor car it might be a wise precaution to preserve a few of these mounting blocks with a view to future use within the next decade or two!

Thatched cottage with window peaks, Thorpe-le-Soken

Mounting block, Bradwell

CHAPTER V

Harbours, Shipyards, Barges, Bridges and Moats

Essex, with a fair proportion of its boundary lapped by an encroaching sea, has a wealth of nautical history and interesting curiosities tucked away in harbours and backwaters. One of the oldest harbours must surely be that of Harwich which can trace its origins way back to pre-Roman times. During World War I it was the base for the old iron-clad battleships, while in World War II it was the scene of a number of exciting engagements; one being the sinking of a "G" type destroyer, H.M.S. Gypsy, the remains of which can still be seen at low tide in the harbour.

A relic of the troubled times with the warring Dutch Fleet is the unique wooden crane which is still preserved today. Used for port and building haulage this piece consists of two wooden wheels 16 ft. in

Double treadmill, Harwich

diameter the inside of which a group of men would tread to give the necessary lifting power. Originally ordered by the Duke of York in 1667 to assist the defences during the Dutch Wars, it was copied from a similar one at Woolwich. It is now the only example of a double tread mill left in the country. When it was offered to the Harwich authorities back in the 1920's a special light railway was built for its removal to the existing site. Another interesting item to be found at this busy cross-channel port and harbour is the ancient Shipyard Bell. Ordered by the Admiralty in 1664 from a Mr. John Darby of Ipswich for use in the Harwich shipyard, this fine old bell is in a good state of preservation. The bell, which carries the crowned C.R. of Charles II, has a rather interesting history for it was nearly lost to the town when sold to a dealer as a piece of scrap metal. Luckily it was rescued by a Mr. P. J. Pybus who had it cleaned and presented to the Corporation of Harwich. Nearby stands a list of the ships built in the yard between 1660–1827.

This particular shipyard was established by Oliver Cromwell and is often mentioned by Pepys the diarist when he served as M.P. for Harwich and Secretary to the Admiralty during the 17th century.

Whilst in Harwich a visit to the now disused pair of light towers should prove interesting, for these ancient structures, rebuilt by Trinity House in 1818, have witnessed many turbulent scenes over the years. One outstanding feature of these towers is the fact that the tallest has nine sides while the other has ten. They last saw service in 1861. Harwich also has connections with Admiral Lord Nelson the famous British naval hero, for on one occasion – August 9th 1801 – he visited the harbour aboard the frigate H.M.S. Medusa.

It is not only the Essex coastline that holds historical attachments, for around the muddy backwaters we find many strange links with the old sailing ship days. Up the Hard at Walton just over the port-side of Hall Lane and down the cinder track, we come to the deep brick and granite harbour, a relic from the days when the Naze saw ships nosing up through the winding mud flats to take on a cargo of iron castings from the iron foundry situated deep in the backwater. Later, during World War I this Hard became a restricted area, for the foundry was then engaged in manufacturing armaments for the Government.

Yet another relic with a long dead harbour is the commemorative tablet to be found mounted in the wall of Beaumont Quay. Built with stone from the old London Bridge in 1832 this harbour was the scene of great activity during the 19th century as the famous Essex barges unloaded their cargoes of bricks, cattle food or fertiliser ready for the

Old shipyard bell, Harwich

Dis-used light tower, Harwich

waiting farmers and builders. A port which still retains its ancient ceremonies is Brightlingsea, a Cinque Port, while at Wivenhoe we find links with World War II. From here came parts of the pre-cast concrete sectional harbour which was floated across the Channel to make up the famous Mulberry Harbour. Taken to the invasion landing points by the Allies they replaced those harbours blown-up and destroyed by the retreating German forces, until the latter could be cleared of mines and rebuilt.

Wherever there are harbours and shipyards there are bound to be ships and boats. A vessel that conjures up the romance of both sea and backwater is the tall masted sailing barges that spread their great brown sails around our Essex coastline. Now, all but a few, are used for the races which are held from Whitsun to September ranging from the Medway, Pin Mill, to the Blackwater and Southend. Of course barge racing is nothing new, for as far back as 1844, they raced all around the Harwich area. In fact Southend's famous annual regatta owes its foundation to a group of interested businessmen and barge owners who in the mid-1800's started to run a series of barge races from that point.

Essex can also claim to have built the finest barges in the world, for with prime, well-seasoned timbers and a deck of Oregon pine topped with a set of sails cut and hand-sewn in a sail maker's loft at Mersea, Brightlingsea or Southend, the old bargee was all set to face foul weather. The cost of such a barge, at the turn of the century, was about

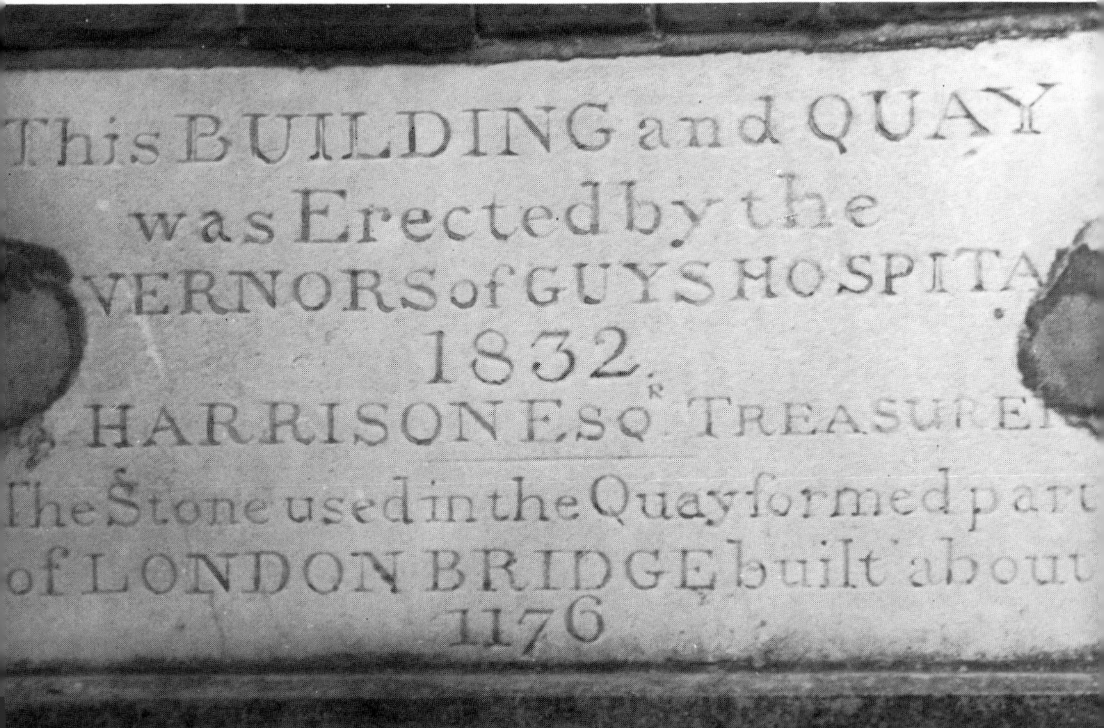

Tablet built from old London Bridge, Beaumont Quay

£1,000. From the yards of Harwich came such famous names as Glen Rosa, Kimberley, Haste Away, Mistley, Freston Tower and the Resolute, which carried out their task of transporting the cement-stone, from the dumps of Harwich to all parts of the country. Up and down the coast and in and out the winding backwaters those great lumbering craft dragged their loads of brick, meal, maize, and acid to out of the way places.

Regular trips were made to such little known places as Landermere, Lower Kirby, Oakley, Beaumont Cut and Walton-on-Naze. From Alresford and St. Osyth they would take sand, while yet on another occasion during the Napoleonic Wars, they unloaded thousands of bricks and mortar on Clacton beaches ready for the masons to build the giant Martello Towers.

Strange stories abound regarding the Essex bargee and his distinctive craft. During the Second World War the Essex barge served well to the fore in the battle front. At Dunkirk they were engaged in bringing troops off the beaches, and among the casualties the "Gertrude May" was lost to a mine in 1942. Other barges served as barrage balloon posts or mine spotting units. Not all tales revolve around the war for some old men recall the time when coal was brought up on the Hard at Maldon where housewives could buy direct at 15s. 0d. per ton. Then again they tell of the hazardous journey up to the wilds of Scotland or across to the ports of Germany, France and Holland. The main harbours for these wooden stalwarts were Harwich, Maldon and Mistley

Old Essex barges, Maldon

and at Mistley the old firm of Horlocks is still going strong, for they can lay claim, as they did in the 18th century, to owning most of the barges in Mistley. Their flag, or bob, as it is called, is a white Maltese cross on a blue field and can be seen flying in the Medway and Thames barge races during the summer months.

A stroll around the stretch of backwater sea wall (Lower Kirby to Walton section), will reveal the derelict hulk of a concrete barge. Although not of the same type as those just mentioned, it was built at the same time as the Mulberry Harbour, and served as an ammunition stores as well as an auxiliary unit for the Mulberry defences. This Essex example has lain slowly sinking into the black mud for some thirty years.

In the area adjacent to the Copperas Bay there was, during the Second World War, a secret project known by the code name of "Sound City". Here, on the wind swept mudflats, a whole town was constructed of prefabricated buildings early in the war by a team of professional scenery manufacturers. Made from wood, tin and inflatable rubber sections, from the air the area resembled a fair sized town. The idea of "Sound City" was that once enemy aircraft had been sighted heading towards the important port of Ipswich, a signal could be flashed to the bogus town where a picked team of men would

Concrete barges, Walton, Relics of Mulberry Harbour scheme

operate lights, traffic and all the necessary paraphernalia of a busy town caught up in the middle of an air raid. Meanwhile back in Ipswich a team of specially trained troops opened up the various smoke making machines thus blanketing the real target with a thick layer of smoke. Although never used in anger, practice runs were made, and the town still remembers the night when the wind changed bringing the choking fumes down into the very town itself.

Leaving the fresh air of coast and backwater one can wander off to explore the selection of bridges that lie scattered in out of the way places. One of the most interesting being the Newport Toll Bridge. Still preserved is the list of charges.

NEWPORT TOLL BRIDGE

TOLL PAYABLE AT THIS GATE

For every Waggon, Van or Cart .... 2d.
For every Horse, Mare, Gelding or Mule, led or driven
(not drawing or rode).. 1d.
For every Ass, led or driven (not drawing or rode) .... ½d.
For every drove of Oxen, Cows, or Neat Cattle per Score .... 4d.
For every Ox, Cow, or herd of Neat Cattle less than a Score .... 1d.
For Sheep and Pigs per Score................................. 4d.
For every Sheep or Pig less than a Score....................... ½d.
For every Bull.. 4d.
Parishes exempt from the payment of Toll:
Newport, Wicken, Saffron Walden, Great Chesterford, Little Chesterford, Wendens Quendon and Widdington.

At Battlesbridge we find a fine example spanning the River Crouch. In the bridge books between 1556 and 1717 there are 47 entries referring to the bridge and its general state of disrepair. The old bridge was finally demolished in 1768 being replaced by a new one in June 1769. Built once again of timber this one cost £457, being 100 ft. long and 8 ft. wide built on a trestle design supported on six unbraced pairs of uprights. Even this did not seem to be satisfactory to the powers that be for a recommendation to enlarge the structure in 1854 was shelved in favour of replacing the whole rickety creation with a bridge of iron costing the grand sum of £1,500.

Although pleasantly designed with a fine unsupported arch of 97 ft. the construction proved too weak, so much so that in June 1871 with a monster steam traction engine, weighing over twelve tons, straddled across its back, the bridge collapsed into the river. The present bridge, built in 1872, was of a far better design and construction boasting three arches. For over a hundred years this bridge has stood the test of time, seeming very little the worse for wear even with the added burden of speeding 20th century traffic.

Crossing the bridge which spans the River Pant at Bocking one should stop and inspect the rather unusual design in the form of a dolphin cast into the lamp standards. The dolphin was the crest of William Courtenay, archbishop from 1381–1396. Back in 1926 the College of Arms granted the Bocking council permission to use a dolphin with raised tail as its armorial bearing. This was the first time in the history of England that a parish council had ventured to apply for a grant of armorial bearings. The history of Bocking is linked with the famous priory of the Holy Saviour at Canterbury which together with the Island of Mersea was made over as a gift to the Benedictine monastery of Canterbury.

Smaller bridges of interest still exist in Essex and among them there is one which dates back to the 13th century. At Little Coggeshall the Long Bridge lies about quarter of a mile west of the chapel and is of three spans and red brick. It was built probably about the 13th century as the brickwork is similar to that employed at the Abbey, although it has been widened on the east side in modern times. The arches are slightly pointed and the cut-waters are additions of doubtful date. At Pleshey there is a fine single span bridge with brickwork of 15th century design. It has a two centre arch crossing the old moat that surrounded the once famous medieval Saxon castle.

The seven arch railway bridge at Brentwood is also of interest for this was built by the old Eastern Counties Railway Company taking four years to complete. It was finished in 1843.

Although much repaired over the years the Elizabethan bridge at Tolleshunt D'Arcy crossing the remains of a moat is well worth a visit as are those to be found at Navestock and Waltham Abbey. The bridge at Navestock is at the side of the remains of Shonk's Mill, about a mile from the church. It is of brick and was probably built in the 17th century. The bridge at Waltham Abbey is about 280 yards from the old church and is of 14th century construction retaining three chamfered ribs forming three central arches.

Moats were all part of our heritage when an Englishman's home was indeed his castle and a moat acted as a defence against marauding bands of itinerate villains and cut throats. Not many have survived the ravages of time and progress and those that are to be found bear very little resemblance to the original structure. At Colchester the moat that

Seven arch bridge, Brentwood

surrounded the Norman castle is nothing more than a pleasantly grassed depression while that which surrounds the Martello Tower at Clacton has been reduced to a children's Toy Town and Zoo. At St. Osyth, embracing the charming 14th century St. Clair's Hall is a very fine example which was formerly divided by a cross-arm.

A place which boasts a number of Homestead Moats is the small parish and village of Sheering just outside Harlow. Although almost non-existent now, there were about five moated areas in this district. Another pair of Homestead Moats are to be found in the small parish of Willingale Spain just 4 miles from Chipping Ongar. One is at the site of the old Rectory while the other is at the site of Minsons. At the turn of the century there were some 211 sites in Essex which boasted moated remains, but now one would be hard pressed to hazard a guess as to how many are left.

CHAPTER VI

Wells, Pumps, Fountains, Stand-Pipes, Horse-Troughs, Dene-Holes

One of Man's prime needs has always been water which together with food and shelter make up his basic requirements. Consequently we find traces of wells, pumps and fountains in most of our villages and old towns. Many are still in working order but others have long since gone, the only thing visible being a small cast iron plaque setting out its history and position. Many riots have raged over the rights to a well or pump comparable only with the range-wars of western America during the mid 19th century.

A fine example of a Norman well is to be found in Colchester Castle. This is 48 feet deep to the shallow depths of the water below and this well is in a fair state of preservation, for when it was inspected by a team of sub-aqua divers a few years ago they discovered an old hunting arrow head and among the numerous coins, a George III penny. Still in Colchester another well, in use up to a few years ago, is to be found in Culver Street and still carries a warning and danger sign.

Traces of other wells, this time of Roman origin are also to be found in Essex and three main examples are at Chigwell, Wanstead and Low Leyton. At Chigwell, in gravel beds about half a mile from Woolston Hall, two wells were discovered during excavations in the 1920's. Both had served as rubbish dumps, and coins and pottery of the Roman period were found. In Wanstead Park the Herony Pond is believed to have originally been a Roman Well, for during excavations in 1715 and 1846, urns, fragments of mosaic pavement and other Roman articles were discovered.

The third example, at Low Leyton, in the region of Grange Park and the Hackney Marshes was also discovered during excavations in 1771 when fragments of oak timbers, numerous Roman coins and "bitts of silver with Saxon characters" were also turned up. A fine old well is also to be found in the sleepy village of Steeple but is no longer in use owing to the installation of main water pipes.

Closely associated with these old wells are the pumps which were usually erected outside the village centre or meeting place. A pump which was erected at Earls Colne by the local townsfolk acts as a commemoration to those who lost their lives in a cholera outbreak which swept Essex during the nineteenth century. Another interesting pump is to be found in the front garden of a cottage in the village of Tendring. Still working and well maintained this cast iron pump used to serve all the village needs before the introduction of piped water.

Yet another pump, which has a history of violence can be found in the Main Street, Great Dunmow. This, it is thought, stood outside the Saracen's Head Hotel, Great Dunmow until the year 1786, when the local authorities decided to fill in the well and remove the old pump. It was deemed to be something of a traffic hazard! Much bitter controversy arose over this issue and the townsfolk who serviced and maintained the pump took umbrage at its removal. So heated did the situation become that the people rose as one and started to remove the stones and earth from the filled-in well. No sooner had they finished than the authorities came along and filled it in again. Three times this was done but eventually the irate protesters managed to clear the well and erected a new pump in August 1786. If they thought they had won the battle they were sadly mistaken for soon the turnpike commissioners and local constable arrived to undo the local blacksmith's good work.

By now tempers had become frayed to the point of an ugly scene breaking out between the lawmen and the angry townsfolk. So casualties occurred on both sides and after the reading of the Riot Act a number of men were arrested and carried off. Taken to the nearest prison they were kept there until their trial at Chelmsford Assizes. Despite vigorous protests from the townspeople who maintained that the authorities had employed professional thugs and bully-boys to carry out their orders of destruction and arrest, the defendants were all found guilty and sent to prison for a period ranging from six months to a year.

During Queen Victoria's long and chequered reign it was common practice to erect fountains around towns and villages for all sorts of occasions. If the British Army fought another successful war in some corner of the far flung Empire then yet another fountain was placed in a strategic position in the town or village square, the details inscribed

Pump commemorating cholera outbreak at Earls Colne, 1853

Village pump in working order, Tendring

on a cast iron plaque.

Classed as one of the oldest working fountains in Essex the magnificent, larger than life swan to be seen at Mistley was the brain-child of Robert Adam the famous architect. Originally designed as part of a sea bathing establishment it would have been capable of furnishing both hot and cold sea water baths, but the only part to be completed was the swan we see today. At Braintree there is a naked boy fountain with the lad disporting himself among the dancing waters, he holds a fish in each hand while an otter at his feet looks hungrily on. At Great Bardfield there is a fountain which was erected in the village in 1860. This served as the village water supply for nearly a century till pipe water was introduced. At Colchester there is a rather grand example near the market which served to quench the thirst of the market folk as they went about their business.

Unfortunately, with so much redevelopment going on and many of the grand old buildings being bulldozed away, a good proportion of these pumps and fountains are being removed.

Stand-pipes, those cast iron relics still to be seen scattered about some Essex towns were all important up to the Second World War.

The Lonely Swan, remains of Robert Adam's hot & cold sea water baths, Mistley

Used by horse drawn water sprinkler carts vital in laying the dust of unmade roads the stand-pipes eliminated the need for countless return journeys back to the main water tower. In Clacton there is a most unusual system of street water supply; here they have drawn on the bottomless depths of the North Sea, and a visit to the seafront to the starboard side of the pier will reveal a strange iron sign post, its head standing above the tossing waves. Looking for all the world like an obsolete "Halt! Major Road Ahead" sign, this old iron post marks the spot for a sea water inlet trap. At the turn of the century, the sea water was pumped from this point with the aid of a gas engine, into the town centre and the reservoir. From here it was led off into a series of stand-pipes situated around the town and outlying district. Householders could rent a brass turn-key from the Town Hall allowing them to draw off their own water for washing or bathing. In the town centre, at St. Osyth Road, a large cast-iron tank was buried beneath the grass verge. When filled with sea water it would swing on an axle to pour its load thus flushing out the sewers and gulleys of the surrounding roads. An old man who had worked at the Town Yard, recalls how they used to climb up the reservoir tower perched high above the town, and sit and cast lines for the fish which had been pumped up from the seashore. All that remains now of this Edwardian sea water scheme is the rusting intake pipe way out in the sea and a few stand-pipes, although the children's boating lake is still fed from the same source.

The Victorian period also saw a great influx of horse and cattle troughs. Once again, just as the ornate fountains had sprung up in gay profusion, the horse trough was erected by well meaning bodies in an attempt to curtail the appalling conditions that befell both horse and horned beast as they trampled through the long dusty roads and tracks. With the onslaught of the motor-car the need for such troughs slowly waned and in most Essex towns the authorities have seen fit to discard them. Not so in Colchester where the troughs have been transformed into rather ornate, giant flower boxes which in summer are a picture of splendid colour. In Rayleigh, when the authorities let it be known that they intended to scrap their trough, which was erected by the Metropolitan Drinking Fountain and Cattle Trough Association a petition was raised and such was the public outrage that it was finally left where it was. Another fine example of a drinking trough of a rather unusual design is to be found just off the London to Harwich road opposite Ramsey church. This long, bath-shaped trough sports cast-iron horses hoofs and legs.

Over the centuries many strange stories have evolved around the

Sea water inlet box, Clacton beach

Sea water stand-pipe, Clacton

series of deep holes sunk into the chalky ground of Hangman's Wood, Grays. Thought to be at least Early Bronze Age period, these pits or dene-holes as they have come to be known have proved very interesting to both layman and scholar alike. During the past 50 years or so a great deal of research has been carried out in and around these holes. One school of thought thinks the ancient tool marks were caused by early man searching for flints while the others plump for a vast grain storage complex arguing that the preservative quality of the chalk would have prevented deterioration of the grain. Yet another group favours the idea of these chambers being places of concealment during times of war. Whatever the explanation, they are certainly well worth a visit for the workmanship carried out as it was, with the crudest of implements, is absolutely first class.

Horse trough with hooves, Ramsey

CHAPTER VII

Almshouses, Schools, Mansions, Cottages, Inns, Guildhalls

Back in the old days almost any village worth its salt boasted a block of almshouses, but today, with a welfare state capable of ministering to the poor, sick and aged many of these fine old buildings have either been demolished or set to some other use.

Almshouses can trace their history back to ancient times and are in fact a direct development of the medieval hospital common in towns and cities, providing free shelter and accommodation not only for the local poor and aged, but for any traveller passing through. The almshouses at the village of Stock built during the reign of Elizabeth I in 1575 were built on the instructions of a local benefactor named Richard Twedye who left money and a piece of land for the erection of four almshouses, "for the comfort of four knights who had fallen on hard times".

Certain instructions were observed when vetting the proposed tenants, one being that poor married couples who were "not given to swearing, drinking, or any other vice" could be eligible for entry.

At Colchester, a 17th century stone tablet records the initial foundation of Finch's Charity during Tudor Times. It is now reset in the wall of the present almshouses.

> "These four Houses Were
> Built & Endowed By Mr
> Ralph Finch in the
> year 1552"

Other interesting almshouses are to be found at Clavering, dating from the 15th century, now a smart farm type house which was

Slate pencil cuts in brickwork on school wall, Wittam

originally five tenements, and Well's Charity, Elsenham, an almshouse founded about 1656, consisting of three tenements being half a mile from the church.

At Saffron Walden we find the Abbey Farm and Almshouses, nearly one mile south-west of the church being partly of one storey, and partly of two storeys. The walls are of brick and the roofs tiled. It was built about 1600 on a double quadrangular plan as an almshouse of twenty tenements, ten in each quadrangle, with a chapel, hall and kitchen in the range between the two quadrangles. At some unknown date the east end of the chapel was pulled down, and in the 19th century the middle range and north quadrangle were considerably altered internally.

Old schools prove of some interest although many have now been replaced by more modern buildings. One, a timber and thatched version is to be found in the village of Beaumont although it has long been empty and disused. Another in Guithavon Street, Witham, bears long cuts in the brickwork by the children's entrance. These were caused by slate pencils as they were hurriedly sharpened before rushing into school. Two schools which have links with a former Archbishop of York are to be found in Chigwell. Samuel Harnett, born in 1561, the son of a humble Colchester baker, eventually rose to become the Archbishop of York and he founded the two schools in 1629. Above the original entrance is a plaque bearing the date and archbishop's mitre.

St. Cedd's Church, Bradwell-on-Sea

In Essex we find a number of barns that in the past have served other curious purposes, but at Bradwell-on-Sea there is a church that became a barn, later to be turned back into a church. Thought to have originally been built by St. Cedd in 654 it was one of the earliest places of worship in England. Although used as a barn until 1920, when it was restored to its original purpose, the building retains much of the original materials. Another unusual barn is that mounted on saddle stones at Little Bardfield on the road between Great Bardfield and Thaxted.

The number of grand old country houses that still retain their original old world elegance and charm are all too few and far between. In Essex a few have come under the cloak of the Department of the Environment and are therefore, in nearly all instances, open to the general public at certain times of the year.

Situated about a mile west of Saffron Walden is the grand old mansion of Audley End. Through successive owners this impressive building has been restored and renovated, but always in keeping with the original style. The name commemorates Sir Thomas Audley who was the Speaker in King Henry VIII's Parliament which suppressed

Mistley Towers, 1776, near Manningtree

the monasteries. For his work the King raised him to the peerage and gave him the site of Walden Abbey. The building of the house was started by a descendant, the Earl of Suffolk, in 1603, and took thirteen years to complete, costing £200,000. About 1720, Vanbrugh was instructed to demolish most of the outer court and to remodel the great hall, although he retained the original richly decorated screen. The first Lord Braybrooke employed Robert Adam to beautify the many apartments, and to create a new suite, the result being the Audley End we know today. Another link with Robert Adam is the Mistley Towers near Manningtree. Home of the playboy squire Richard Rigby it was the scene of some rather wild parties and among the famous guests were David Garrick the actor and Francois de la Rochefoucauld. Squire Rigby engaged the services of Robert Adam, the famous architect, to design Mistley Towers in 1776. While on the subject of Towers a visit to the Layer Marney Towers near Colchester is well worth a trip. Described as the most ambitious gatehouse in England this eight storey gatehouse tower was begun early in the 16th century by Henry, 1st Lord Marney, but at the time of his death in 1523, and that of his son in 1524, the building was left incomplete and has never been finished. It was restored during the present century when gaps between the gatehouse and the east wing were filled in. This gatehouse has moulded string courses between the storeys, an embattled parapet and square turrets at the angles with trefoiled corbel-tables and traces of former cresting. Each turret has seven two-light windows in the return wall, while the gatehouse has six chimney-shafts all with moulded bases. An outstanding feature of this Tudor brickwork is the terracotta dolphin-crestings.

Stanway, on the London to Colchester road, derives its name from the Roman road "Stone Way" which was used by the chariots and heavy supply waggons and along this busy road we find the impressive Stanway Hall. This was built during the reign of King Henry VIII on the site of the original manor of King Harold, but after his tragic death at the Battle of Hastings in 1066, passed to William I. Inside the Hall, one room is lined with early 17th century panelling. It also contains an original stone fireplace with scrolled foliage, small figures and a cartouche. Yet another fine house is that of Moyns Park near Steeple Bumpstead, once a moated house and named after its original owner, Robert de Fitz William le Moigne. The house can be traced back to the beginning of the 14th century. Among the many owners the most notable was Thomas Gent who under the guidance of Sir Francis Walsingham, Secretary of State during the reign of Elizabeth I, was

Layer Marney Towers, near Colchester. The most ambitious gatehouse in England

responsible for uncovering numerous plots to assassinate the Queen.

Another house that had links with Elizabeth I is Gosfield Hall near Halstead, a most imposing mansion dating in part from the 15th century. During the reign of Henry VII it would appear to have been a brick house built around a quadrangle on to which all the windows looked, the outside being of plain windowless walls. The house was owned successively by de Veres, Rolfes and the Wentworths. The Wentworth heiress married Sir Hugh Roch, the second son of Lord Chancellor Roch, and after her husband's death Lady Roch was twice visited by Queen Elizabeth while the Queen carried out an inspection of her troops and ships in Essex. Except for the Tudor Gallery the house was rebuilt in 1705, and a century later it was inhabited for seven years by King Louis XVIII of France.

A rather unique building is Beeleigh Abbey just one mile west of Maldon. This abbey has the distinction of being one of the few religious houses with rooms restored almost to their original condition. Built during the 12th century, it belonged to the order of Premonstratesian of White Canons.

The abbey as it remains today consists of a larger part of the cloister court on the east side, which includes the chapter house, with the dormitory above the calefactory or warming house. There is also a portion of some buildings on the south side. The library contains many fine and rare books some dating back to the 15th century. In the James Bedroom is a beautiful carved bed made for King James I about 1605, a really superb piece of furniture. There are some very fine 13th century painted glass windows showing religious motifs which should not be missed.

Back to the picturesque setting of St. Osyth we find in St. Osyth Priory a building which dominates the entire village. This was the home of Saint Osyth, daughter of the first King of the East Angles, who founded the nunnery at Chich, by which name it was originally known. She was beheaded by the Danes in 663 and it has become local legend that her ghost walks the lonely back-road on the night of the full moon. During the Civil War the priory was raided by Parliamentary troops, searching for escaping Royalists.

Robert de Belmeis founded the Priory about 1253, the ruins of which we see today together with the well preserved Gatehouse which was restored during the 15th century. The earliest remaining work is the sub-vault of the Dorter range which is of the same period as the foundations; the still existing portions of the wall bounding the Cloister on the north and west are possibly also of this date. The Priory, or

St. Osyth Priory Gatehouse

Abbey was suppressed in 1539 and in 1553 came into the possession of Lord Darcy who transformed the buildings into a house, destroying some parts and making additions in others. At the same time the church, which flanked the cloister was completely destroyed. Above the main archway we find a large oriel window, modern externally, except for the moulded and carved head and the panelled and carved base and corbelling. The head has a band of early Renaissance ornament with foliage and small nude figures. A number of shields contain various devices of Abbot Vintoner, St. Osyth, Tunstall bishop of London, Henry VIII, later arms of the Abbey – parted chevronwise, in chief a ring between a mitre and a crozier – and the arms of Bourchier.

It is not only the grand houses of Essex that carry stories of historical interest for a number of the old farmhouses and cottages could tell many a hair-raising story if those old timbers could only talk. At Ash Farm, Weeley, we find a farmhouse which had close links with the Napoleonic Wars. Serving as an officer's quarters during the early 1800's Ash Farm was the scene of several wild parties as officers entertained the local gentry and their lady friends. One such party, which lasted for nearly a week, became the talk of the district for among the guests was the Prince Regent and his entourage. This was sponsored and laid on by the local Squire Weeley. Just how successful this ball proved can be judged by the fact that the squire ended up in a debtors' prison the next year. Squire Weeley's militia sword and tunic can be seen in Colchester Castle Museum.

During alterations to this old house in the 1960's a small cupboard was discovered in a chimney breast beneath layers of encrusted wall-paper. Inside lay a 16 bore flintlock, officer's holster pistol by Blake of London, circa 1803.

Some houses sport strange decorations but none could be more curious than the house known as "Dragons" situated on a hill overlooking Loughton. Built in 1883 on the instructions of Henry Marshall Fletcher, a well-to-do ship builder, the house is completely dominated by dragons. Everywhere the eye reaches one is surrounded by dragons in wood, plaster and even copper. Inside and out dragons stand, stoop or crouch in gay profusion.

Treasure Holt, haunted farmhouse, Burrsville

No self respecting ancient house would admit to not possessing a ghost or two and a farm cottage which can boast an assortment of spooks is Treasure Holt at Burrsville. Not only have they been seen by the owner and members of his family but as far back as the 1920's the Psychic Research Society verified suspicions that spirits were on the move in that cottage. The whole atmosphere of Treasure Holt vibrates with a strange aura for entering this building is like turning back the pages of history and disturbing the ghosts of the past. There are no luxuries here of gas or electricity; only the humble candle and oil lamp serve to light the low beamed rooms. The history of this cottage dates back to the 14th century and during the heyday of smugglers it was used as a headquarters by local free-booters. Here on the road at the back of beyond smugglers used to bring their booty from the marshes where it had been landed by the long boats under the very noses of the excise men. In the 18th century the Essex coastline was a regular hide-out for smuggling activities. Along the coastline from Harwich, Walton, Brightlingsea and far beyond, excise men tried in vain to stop the loads of brandy, tobacco, and bales of silk from reaching their eventual destination. Many times a running battle was fought between the excise men and members of the "brotherhood". Records show that the law men were very often left to fend for themselves, many dying during the long night, their cries being completely ignored by local villagers. Little wonder that the excise man went about his task with a faint heart. If he was killed during the course of his duty his widow and children were awarded the magnanimous sum of £7 10s and £1 10s respectively.

Partial evidence as to who or what the spirits may have been was uncovered in the spring of 1928. During repairs to the floor in the main room, workmen stumbled across a small cache of interesting oddments; a bone comb, three buckles, three clay pipes, a copper token, a few fragments of bone, two rusty finger rings and a shattered metal coat button. Investigation on these objects placed them around the date line of 1790 for the bone comb is identical to those carved by French prisoners of war who were encamped and worked around Harwich and district during the French Wars, while the token is also of that period. The fragments of bone have been identified as being human finger bones.

What exactly happened at that old farm on a dark and lonely night back in those far-off restless days one can only surmise, but whatever it was, be it the discovery of a peeping excise man or perhaps a drunken quarrel among men of the brotherhood, those fragments of bone and buckles from shoe or hat did not join the other items under the floor boards by sheer accident. We know for a fact that this farm was used for smuggling so it would be safe to assume that whoever stomps around the rooms of Treasure Holt could well have been "turned-off" after an evening's lucrative trip over the marshes.

A number of these old places sport barge-boards, a board often carved and fixed to the edge of a gabled roof a short distance from the face of the wall. Examples of these may be found on the Green Man Inn at Bran End, Stebbing, and at Little Brockhold's Farm, Radwinter. Another 15th century example can be found on the barn at Prior's Hall, Widdington.

Leaving Colchester via the steep East Hill one mounts the old bridge spanning the ancient River Colne, a river which has witnessed many strange happenings and a great number of chapters of history unfold. Lying snug against the old flour mill can be found the Siege House complete with peppered, weather-beaten timbers. Thought to be of late 15th century or early 16th century origin this fine old house was utilised as a guardhouse during the siege of 1648 and during one notable skirmish when Royalists tried to break through the barricades,

The Old Siege House, showing ringed bullet holes, Colchester

the timbers received a fair number of lead musket and pistol balls. Today, these holes are still to be seen ringed with red metal markers. Just how much striking power those old muzzle-loaders possessed can be judged by the following anecdote. A young ensign on duty at the Mill was shot through the body, in at one side and out the other, with a five pound bullet from a heavy wall gun. He went from his guard to his quarters in the heart of the town, by the help of one soldier only, who led him, the bullet hanging by his side in the skin. The missile broke out at last when he lay down on his bunk to die. A number of houses have links with the siege but the Old Siege House is the most prominent of all.

Houses which sport strange and peculiar curiosities pop up from time to time and such is the case with the odd little trap door to be seen halfway up the wall of Foulkbourne Post Office. In the days of horse drawn mail vans the early morning mail was delivered at 4 a.m. and rather than leave his bed the village postmaster hit upon the novel idea of having a shutter built into the bedroom wall next to his bed, so he could take personal delivery.

When we witness the present day concrete monstrosities rising up almost over night we seem to think of concrete as something fairly modern but as far back as 1873 houses were being built of that material. Down Hall, at Hatfield Broad Oak, originally owned by Matthew Prior, poet and diplomatist, was demolished and rebuilt in 1871-73 and was in fact one of the first concrete houses erected in England. Designed by Cockerill, it was built in the Italian style.

Moving house is a fairly demanding job at the best of times but the Moot Hall, Clacton must surely take the prize for the biggest move to be made in Essex. Built in 1690 as a dower house in the grounds of Horstead Place near Bury St. Edmunds, the property was demolished in 1910 to be taken by a fleet of horse drawn waggons to its present site. With all parts numbered and listed the giant task of rebuilding it all began. When a staircase was added in 1934 the owners saw fit to employ a gang of navvies to thrash around the ancient timbers with hob-nailed boots to give an air of wear-and-tear.

Essex is famous for its weather-boarded cottages and in fact in America similar ones were erected by the Pilgrim Fathers known as "frame houses". At Billericay we find the old Chantry House, assembly point of the Essex contingent of the Pilgrim Fathers under the leadership of Christopher Martin. Martin was appointed governor of the "Mayflower", the ship which took them across the wild seas to a new life. On the subject of timber framed houses a rather unusual

Trap door in wall of Post Office, Foulkbourne

Moot Hall, Clacton

cottage is to be found in Rowlands Yard, Dovercourt. Here we find a dwelling known as Number One, Deck House. It was built entirely from the decking and timbers of a wrecked ship, the stairs and ceilings all bear traces of its former life with hooks and eyelets hanging from the beams. Even the ceiling timbers are caulked just like a ship, and instead of normal windows it was furnished with port-holes.

One of the finest houses in Essex must surely be Paycocke's House, Coggeshall. It is rated as one of the best preserved examples of a 16th century merchant's house in the country. Built by a family of rich clothiers, this fine old building has been kept in a good state of repair. The house consists of two storeys, timber-framed and partly plastered, with a tiled roof. At the back of the house are two wings, the south-east one being the oldest, the one on the south-west being of late 16th century period with a 17th century extension on the south side.

The north front has exposed timber-framing with modern brick filling. The upper storey projects, and the carved facia board is ornamented with foliage, small heads and figures, and a shield with a merchant's mark of an ermine tail, and the initials T.P. – Thomas Paycocke. Both storeys of the house are divided into five bays by restored buttresses supporting curved brackets. Inside the house in the south wall is a fireplace with carved animals, and yet another shield bearing the merchant's mark, and scrolls bearing the name Thomas Paycocke. The walls display some beautiful linen-fold panelling of unique design.

At the quaint little village of Matching Tye we find a rather unique two storey building known as the Marriage Feast Room. Built some 500 years ago it was, and still is used for its original purpose. It is rather noteworthy as one of the few surviving buildings of this class.

With Good Queen Bess dominating the Essex scene so much it seems only fitting to visit the tranquil setting of Epping Forest. Here we find a grand old Tudor building known as Queen Elizabeth's Hunting Lodge. Originally designed as an open framed building from which the non-participants could watch their hunting friends and comrades enjoy themselves, it was a favourite spot of the Queen. Today it houses a

Old Chantry House, home of the Pilgrim Fathers, Billericay

Paycock's House, Coggeshall, 16th century merchant's house

small museum of forest and hunting curios and is under the care and protection of the City of London authorities.

Old inns seem to have a fascination of their own and in Essex many seem to boast ties with that highwayman of all highwaymen, Dick Turpin. True he ranged all over Essex from the Isle of Canvey to Colchester, and up around the woods and hills of Loughton, and because most of his "listening-posts" were in the local village inns he must have visited a fair number during his hectic and exciting career in the early part of the 18th century. Inns he is known to have frequented are at Hempstead, his birthplace, and the old Black Lion at Epping.

I suppose that because of the association with local inns, condemned highwaymen and footpads were executed from a tree nearest to an inn and the crossroads. Not only did it act as a worthwhile deterrent to other would-be villains but it was thought to prevent the damned soul from wandering in search of those responsible for his untimely demise.

Besides being hung at the crossroads the dead felon was left to swing in chains from the gibbet, later to be cut down and buried upright in the middle of the crossing. Such must have been the case of the poor soul who haunts the dark lanes near "The Fusiliers", Little Bentley. A number of folk have witnessed the ghostly apparition which gallops on a large white horse down the leafy country lanes.

An inn with close connections with the old stage coaching days is the Swan Inn at Stratford. As far back as 1788 there was an hourly short-stage coach service to Whitechapel from this inn, and by 1821 the coaches ran from between 9 a.m. and 10 p.m. each day.

Stories of spies and foreign agents always set the imagination agog and at the "Black Boy", Weeley we find the setting for the real live thing. During World War I the inn was the haunt of one, Ernest Henry Bourneman, a gentleman who had purchased the old Weeley Mill in 1913 on the pretext of the furtherance of his artistic studies. On the outbreak of the war Bourneman could be seen, seated at the "Black Boy" armed with sketch-block and pencils. Here he would execute

15th century Guildhall, Thaxted

lightning sketches of troops and vehicles and was often to be found wandering around camps and installations at the nearby garrison town of Colchester. Later it was established that the man was in fact a German spy. Although arrested and charged it was found that the artist who lived in the Weeley windmill was an American citizen although he had seen service in the Imperial German Army at the turn of the century. Once back in the States Bourneman produced a series of articles on his adventures, writing at some length about his stay in Weeley.

Known as the "Sheffield of East Anglia" Thaxted has one of the most photographed buildings in Essex. The ancient Guildhall situated at the head of Town Street just 100 yards south-east of the church is thought to have been built in the second half of the 15th century and restored early in the 18th century when the present tiled roof was put on. Originally built as a Cutler's Hall, Thaxted being the main centre for the medieval sword and knife industry, this fine old building is classed as one of the few remaining ancient Guildhalls in Britain. There are three other Guildhalls in Essex, one now the parish hall at Finchingfield, another at Ashdon reduced to three tenements, and last but not least the remains of a Guildhall at Moreton now used as a cottage.

For those who wish to visit the grand old houses of Essex the following should prove of some use:

Paycocke's House. (National Trust). Coggeshall. Open: Easter Day until the end of September, Bank Holiday Mondays and every Wednesday, Thursday and Sunday, 2 to 5.30 p.m.

Audley End Mansion. (Ministry of Public Buildings and Works). 1 mile west of Saffron Walden, on the A.11 Open: Daily 11.30 to 5.30 p.m. April to early October. Closed on Good Friday.

Gosfield Hall. (Mutual Household Associated). 5 miles south of Castle Hedingham. Open: Wednesdays and Thursdays from May to September, 2 to 5 p.m.

Bradwell Lodge. (Tom Driberg, M.P.). Near north end of River Blackwater, off B.1021. Open: Easter to mid-September Wednesdays and Saturdays, 3 to 6 p.m. Bank Holiday Sunday and Monday 3 to 6 p.m.

Castle House. (Lady Munnings). Three-quarters of a mile from Dedham village. Open: End of May to mid-October. Sundays 2 to 4-30 p.m.

Spains Hall. (see further details in chapter ten) renowned for its ornate

Ornate drain pipes, Spains Hall, Finchingfield

drain-pipes.

Hedingham Castle. (Miss Musette Majendie, C.B.E. and Dr Margery Blackie). In Castle Hedingham on the B.1058. Open: Easter Monday 10 to 6 p.m. May to September, Tuesdays, Thursdays and Saturdays 2 to 6 p.m. Spring and August Bank Holiday Mondays 10 to 6 p.m.

Shire Hall. Chelmsford. Open: Most normal working hours and days.

St. Osyth Priory. (Somerset de Chair). Just west of St. Osyth village. Open: Gatehouse – August only, 2 to 4.30 p.m.

Beeleigh Abbey. (Mrs Foyle). 1 mile west of Maldon. Open : All the year, Wednesdays 2 to 5 p.m.

Coggeshall Abbey. (Mr R. M. Brew). The ruins of this abbey may be seen standing on the banks of the River Blackwater. Visitors may look round the Abbey (excluding the private part of the house), by making an appointment with the owner.

Stanway Hall. (Frank and Helena Farrar). 3 miles from Colchester on the B.1022. Open: 9 a.m. to 9.30 p.m. every day.

CHAPTER VIII

Church Curiosities, Lock-ups and Stocks

The only places which stand undisturbed by the pace of progress are the churches. Slumbering on through the centuries they house a mass of interesting information as well as a collection of curiosities. Where else could we find relics of the 11th, 12th and 13th centuries still relatively intact and undisturbed apart from those pieces housed in our national museums and galleries.

For those interested in details of armour and dress a visit to the following churches will be most rewarding. In Little Dunmow Church the effigy of Walter Lord Fitzwalter depicts the type of heavy armour worn by knights in the 14th century. Note the large gardes de bras, at elbow, tuilles, thigh plates and collar of mail at throat. Another, a knight of the Elizabethan period, John, first Lord Petre, can be seen in Ingatestone church wearing richly decorated armour topped with a large ruff and covered with a lined cloak. Sir Thomas Smith in Theydon Mount Church also wears armour of the Elizabethan period. Most outstanding feature is his "peasecod" breast-plate so synonimous with the late 16th century. One of the most detailed pieces is that of Sir Henry Mayhard in Little Easton Church. Every detail even down to hooks, eyes, straps and rivets has been faithfully reproduced. Note the countless number of folds on the ruff. The effigy of Sir Denner Strutt can be viewed in Little Warley Church, dressed in half-plate armour similar to that worn during the Civil War. Laminated thigh plates, fully articulated, earned them the nickname of "lobster tails". Sir Roger Wentworth in Wethersfield Church wears a tabard, a loose type of coat with short stiff sleeves. Note the coutiers protecting the elbows.

Essex is renowned for its churches and the numerous carved memorials found therein. At Little Horkesley the church, which was bombed during World War II and now re-built, contains several wooden effigies and some splendid brasses including the famous Swynborne brasses. Essex is also noted for wooden effigies and an interesting selection can be found at Danbury, Little Baddow and Elmstead.

A rather unusual memorial is that in St. Nicholas's Church, South Ockendon, erected by Lady Susanna Saltonstall in memory of her husband, Sir Richard, who died in 1601 aged 80. Sir Richard was a Lord Mayor of London and a member of the Skinner's Company of London. Another example can be found in the church of Willingale and Spain for this is made of wood and parchment. It records the six sons of Edward Bewsy who lived and died during the 17th century.

> "Six lie here, shaken from the tree.
> Where eagles frequent are,
> Dead bodies be."

Many famous families lie buried in Essex and their own individual monuments can be traced from generation to generation. Despite the vandalistic outburst during the Civil War when Parliamentary troops carried out a barbaric plan of destruction on all Royalist property, including tombs and memorials, most of them are still intact, although a few do sport shorn noses, toes, ears, and the odd hand or two. The memorial to Sir John Deane, deputy lieutenant and J.P. for Essex, in Great Maplestead Church, is dated 1625 and depicts the reclining, full size figure of Sir John clad in plate armour. Above on a shelf are the kneeling figures of his widow, two sons and four daughters.

Wooden burial effigy, Elmstead Church

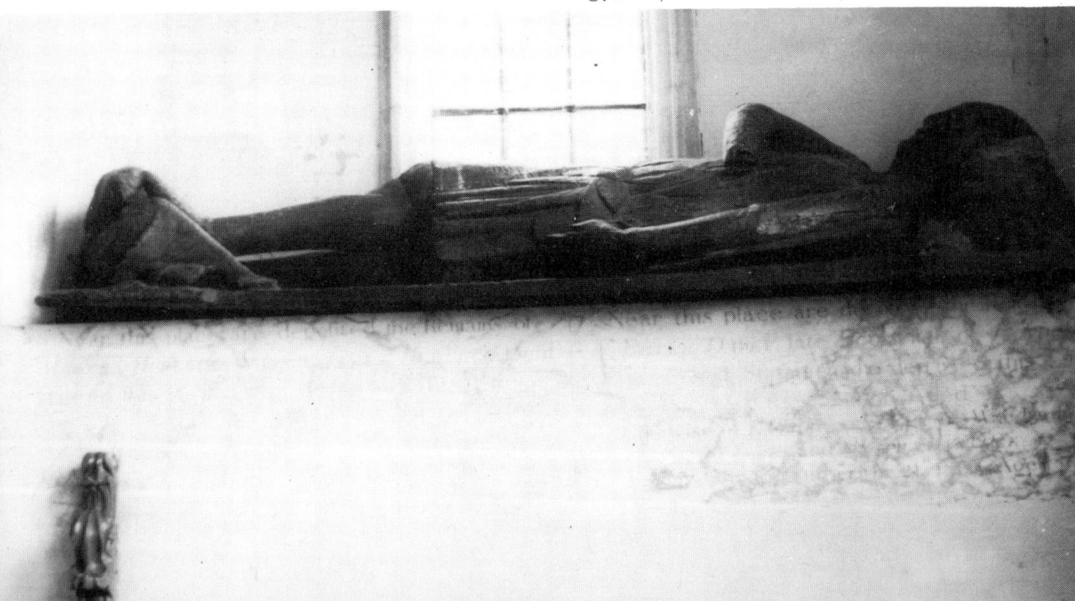

A whole collection of family memorials are in the chancel chapel of North Ockendon. These are to the Pointz family who could lay claim to the distinction of having landed with William the Conqueror.

Although now largely removed for security reasons a few funeral or mortuary helmets, swords and banners are still to be found in some Essex churches. In the past it was custom to display a dead knight's arms in the local church and those to be seen show great age and neglect. Metal is thick with centuries of unchecked rust while the banners hang in tattered, faded shreds. A helmet in a fair state of preservation can be found in the parish church of Great Bardfield. Of 17th century period, it belonged to the Lumley family.

Many strange things exist in churches and not always in full view of the public. At All Saint's Church, East Horndon, beneath the altar-tomb of the Tyrell chapel, according to ancient legend lies the severed head of Ann Boleyn. It is thought to have been smuggled away to this last resting place soon after Ann's execution at the Tower of London in 1536.

In the picturesque church at Danbury, famous for a collection of ornate, carved animals on the bench-ends we find the story of the body found preserved in a strange liquid. What better than quote the letter which appeared in the *Gentleman's Magazine* for 1789 referring to an event of 1779:

> "As some workmen were digging a grave in the north aisle . . . just beneath a niche . . . wherein is placed the effigy of a man in armour . . . they discovered . . . beneath a very massy stone, a leaden coffin without any inscription. Judging that this enclosed the body of the Knight Templar . . . the rector and church-warden resolved to open the coffin.
>
> On raising the lead, there was . . . an elm coffin enclosed . . . very firm and entire. It was found to enclose a shell about three-quarters of an inch thick. The lid of this shell being taken off, we were presented with a view of the body laying in a liquor or pickle resembling mushroom catchup. . . . As I never possessed the sense of smelling and was willing to ascertain the flavour of the liquor, I tasted; and found it to be aromatic, though not very pungent partaking of the taste of catchup and of the pickle of Spanish olives. The body was tolerably perfect. . . . The flesh, except on the face and throat appeared exceedingly white and firm. . . . The body was covered with a shirt of linen; the stitches were very evident, and attached very strongly. . . . There was no hair on the head, nor do I remember any in the liquor, though

Carved bench ends, Danbury Church

Carved bench ends, Danbury Church

Carved bench ends, Danbury Church

Carved bench ends, Danbury Church

feathers, flowers and herbs in abundance were floating – the leaves and stalks of which appeared quite perfect. . . . When the jaws were opened, they exhibited a set of teeth perfectly white. . . . Whether the legs were crossed . . . must forever remain in doubt, though I am strongly of the opinion that they were, for one of the gentlemen pushing a walking stick from the knees to the ankles, the left foot separated from the leg. . . . The whole body conveyed the idea of hearty youth, not in the least emaciated by sickness. The whole length of the corpse very little exceeded 5 feet. The church doors were opened, and the parishioners having satisfied their curiosity, the shell and coffins were again soldered and the whole left . . . in statu quo. . . ."

Among the many interesting items to be found in our churches are the organs. One, in the church of St. Nicholas, can lay claim to having been brought from the chapel of St. Paul's after the Great Fire of

London. It is believed that Milton may have played on it during his career. Another item, famous throughout the world is the "Dunmow Flitch Chair". Housed in Little Dunmow Church it was once used to "chair" the couple who won the famous flitch trial by successfully establishing their claim that they had not quarrelled since their wedding, the victors winning a flitch of prime bacon. The trial was first held in the full procedure of a Norman court during the reign of Henry III.

Chairs, stools and even candlesticks should not be overlooked whilst searching for curiosities for even the candlestick in Harlow Church can be traced back to the year 1697, while the candlebox in Belchamp Walter Church of wood, with top and back covered with metal is dated 1673. A link with those who perished during the Great Plague of 1684 is hand written on the parchment roll preserved in the north chapel of Braintree Church.

Yet another church which boasts carved bench-ends is at Wendens Ambo. One which carries an interesting story is that carved in the form of a tiger. Linked with medieval times, it tells of a hunter who rides off with the cub of a tigress. In pursuit the tigress was delayed by the mirrors the hunter threw down behind him, for as she looked into each mirror in turn and saw her own reflection she thought it was that of her cub. This way the chase was checked and the hunter escaped. The moral of this story is that the Hunter is the Devil, who would seize our souls (the cub) while the mirrors represent the pleasures of this world which stop us from regaining our souls.

Many of the churches have carved beams and doors usually depicting local legends. On the 500 year old church door at Littlebury there is a pair of carved shears symbolic of the wool trade from which the village once prospered. On a beam at St. Andrew's, Greensted, a church built in Saxon times of split logs and being the only wooden church left in Europe, there is a fine carving known as St. Edmunds beam which tells a stirring tale of the young martyred King Edmund. Edmund, first patron saint of England, succeeded to the throne at the age of fifteen being crowned on Christmas Day 855. When he was twenty-nine his army was defeated by the Danish captain Hinguar, who offered to allow Edmund to retain half his kingdom as a vassal state providing he renounced Christianity and worshipped a Danish god. Refusing such terms Edmund was martyred. Legend has it that the tree against which he is said to have been killed fell down in 1839 and a Danish type arrow-head was discovered embedded in the crumbling timbers. Legend also has it that after his death his head was struck off and thrown into the undergrowth. When, the next day,

Edmund's followers found it they saw a large grey wolf standing guard over the grisly relic. The saint was buried and left in peace until 1010 when his remains were taken to London. Three years later the relics were taken to Bury St. Edmunds, his body resting overnight in Greensted Church. Also at this church is a "leper's squint", a small roughly hewn aperture where a stoup of holy water was placed for lepers. It is located on the north side of the nave.

A number of churches in the county boast wood carvings and similar examples to that above can be viewed in the 13th century church at Broxted, between Stansted and Thaxted.

Most churches possess quite distinctive trunks or chests and in fact a worthwhile study could be made of these alone. Scattered around the churches of Essex lie several fine interesting chests, which were, and sometimes still are, used to store church hangings and the vestments of the clergy.

One of the most picturesque is that in Newport parish church. Thought to be a portable altar, legend has it that it was carried by Henry Percy, Earl of Northumberland, on a campaign in France in 1513. An account of this chest reads: "A coffer with two lids, to serve

13th century portable altar, Newport Church

for an altar, if need be, the overlid painted with a crucifix, Mary and John, a superb altar cloth and vestment, and all the other stuff to be put in the said coffer". Each of the painted panels inside the lid forming the reredos show a figure beneath a trefoiled arch – St. Peter, St. John, St. Paul, the Blessed Virgin and, centralized, the crucifixion. They are the earliest known oil paintings on wood known to English art. The chest also has a false bottom to conceal the altar stone.

At Debden we find a 14th century iron bound oak chest thought to be one of the best in the county, while at Stisted there is an early plank built chest with covered lid. An early dugout chest at Little Sampford Church, 4 miles from Thaxted, is made from a whole log, a slice having been sawn off the top to act as a lid.

Arkesden	17th century domestic type hutch, with incised pattern.
Wicham	15th century Flemish chest covered with sheet iron.
Hadstock	Date unknown, of oak long low, and iron bound which was used to keep funeral torches in.
Finchingfield	Late 16th or early 17th century chest with panelled and inlaid front and ends. Whilst in this church note the unusual square tower restored in memory of Daniel Shed, one of the original Pilgrim Fathers who ventured to America in 1640.
Copford	14th century parish chest with two locks, eight staples and a cut in the top for Poor Relief Offerings.
Steeple Bumpstead	Fine example of a 16th century alms box.
Margaret Roding	14th century oak chest, iron bound with early iron ornamentation.
Littlebury	16th century "Poor man's chest" with original slot lid.
Dovercourt	"Poor man's chest" in fine condition bearing the date 1589.
Little Canfield, near Dunmow	13th century chest, most unusual, having broad boards as feet.

Closely associated with chests are the exquisitely carved lecterns – usually executed in the form of a Roman eagle – which carry the unweildy, mammoth antique Bibles. One which deserves special men-

14th century parish poor chest, Copford Parish Church

tion is the 16th century example in St. Botolph's, Hadstock. This is of finely carved oak with a carved stem enriched with a form of cable moulding, cusped and incised foot, and is mounted on an octagonal base.

Until 1840, when the police were finally established in Essex, every parish was compelled by law to provide a lock-up to house local villains and wrong-doers. Over the years many of these buildings have fallen into disrepair or have been demolished but others have stood the change of time and have become symbols of the lawless past. At Bradwell-juxta-Mare the brick built cage also sports a set of oak whipping-posts. Built in 1817 at a cost of £3 10s. 9d., this lock-up is capable of housing half a dozen prisoners. At Canewdon there is also a lock-up together with a set of stocks and a whipping-post. The head post of the stocks bears the date 1775 and a rather unusual feature is the fact these stocks could take three offenders at once instead of the usual two. There are also the marks of an attempt to saw through the wood, but the later addition of iron banding foiled further attempts.

At Great Bardfield on the B1057 next to a house named Cage

Stocks and whipping post, Havering-Atte-Bower

Whipping post, Good Easter

The Lion's Den, Great Holland

Cottage is another lock-up. This is divided into sections so that the sexes could be separated when the occasion arose.

Of course, the grandfather of all Essex lock-ups is the ready-made prison of old Colchester Castle whose damp dungeons housed criminals and wrong-doers up to 1835. On show in the cells are the handcuffs, chains and shackles still to be seen bolted to the cold, damp granite floors. It was here that the Colchester Martyrs were kept prior to execution, while those felons awaiting transportation to Australia and other far-flung dominions also left their marks on the cell-walls.

CHAPTER IX

Inn, Trade, and Road Signs, Wall Ornaments, Fire-Plates, Parge-work, Corbels, Stained Glass Windows

British pubs and inns are steeped in history and tradition and Essex inns are no exception. Although the first known reference to inn signs can be traced back to the ancient Egyptians it was to the Romans that we owe the honour for hanging signs in general. The most popular was their tavern-sign the "Bush" while another was the ansa, or handle of a jug.

As time went by it became common practice to hang a picture of either the local lord, villain, King or Queen, or in fact anything connected with local legend, for in those days of widespread illiteracy words would have meant very little to the uneducated yeoman.

One historian has said, "Tenants of taverns in the old days were often the retired stewards from some ancient house either of the church, the state or nobility and landed gentry, therefore it was only natural for them to desire to show their connection with the powers of their day by painting on their signboards a crest or coat of arms, or even the prominent tincture of the heraldic shield to signify their close association with the prominent person. This is the cause of so many signs having a colour prefix such as the Golden Lion, the Blue Lion, the Red Lion, etc." Many of the signs were thought up as puns or rebuses and not a few were named after their original owners, such as the Wake Arms near Epping. This was named after the Wake family, who were landowners in the area and who claimed descent from Hereward the Wake, the Saxon patriot who defied the Normans long after the rest of the country had accepted their rule.

One of the most popular inn signs in the country must be "Prince of Wales' Feathers". Originally worn by the Black Prince in battle, the white ostrich plume is said to have been worn with the motto "No force alters their fashion" or in modern parlance "Don't get your feathers ruffled". Another couple of signs with Richard III overtones is the "White Rose" which was very popular during his reign but upon his death was very quickly repainted to any other colour but white, and the sign of the "White Boar".

A "White Boar" which was changed to the "Blue Boar" can be found at Maldon, for this inn was originally the 14th century home of the de Veres.

A "Red Lion" which is steeped in history is that at Colchester. Its history is recorded from 1529. Originally built circa 1400 as a private mansion it was converted to an inn around 1500. Until recently it was possible to examine the lead musket balls still embedded in the porch timbers, relics of the bitter fighting during the Siege of 1648.

Many inn signs have been altered over the years and in so doing have lost all their meaning. The "Lion's Den", Great Holland, was in fact yet another "Red Lion" but owing to a whim of a former tenant sports the unusual sign of a lion playing a game of draughts.

Others reflect local interest either in work or play. At Layer-de-la-Haye we find the "Donkey and Buskins". Buskins were a form of leggings favoured by labourers before the introduction of the wellington boot.

Many have links with religious fables. Such being the case of the "Fountain Head", Brentwood. It is said, that when the martyr St. Paul had his head struck off it bounced three times, and a fountain sprang up at each spot it touched.

An inn with a most unusual pun is the "Half Butt Inn" at Great Horkesley, and the "Gun Inn", Gun Hill, Dedham, is also aptly named. A sign, hand carved in oak and over 100 years old, is of the "Spread Eagle" at Little Bardfield. Taken from the arms of the Holy Roman Emperors, many Continental, Russian and old English families bore these arms. The "Maypole Inn" at Tiptree is a typically English inn. It was built alongside the site where the pagan rites of spring were enacted. It is said by one priest "of tenne maydens which went to fetch May, nine of them came home with childe".

At Maldon a number of unique inn signs are to be found around the High Street, many having decorative wrought-iron work surrounding each painted panel.

No finer tribute could be made to that rogue of all rogues Dick Turpin than the sign "Dick Turpin's Birth Place" hanging outside the "Rose & Crown" at Hempstead. Born here in the year 1705 the old inn is known the world over as "Dick Turpin's Inn" rather than by its

An original maypole, serving as a road sign, Tolleshunt D'Arcy

The Black Boy, Weeley, originally a tobacconist's sign

proper title. At Sewardstone, a small inn called "Dick Turpin's Cave" commemorates the cave where that king of the highwaymen used to hide when being pursued by Bow Street Runners.

When in Stock a visit to the "Bear Inn" will not go unrewarded. Here, beneath the arms of the Earl of Warwick is an inn with a very amusing story. Years ago, back in Queen Victoria's day there lived an ostler who was known as "Old Spider". Well renowned for his love of the bottle he would cause untold merriment among the locals by nipping up one chimney and in a while reappear down another in a different part of the inn. Entertaining for those who knew of his party piece but rather disconcerting for unwary customers visiting the place for the first time. It was nothing for the old chap to disappear for a week or more only to materialize again once the effects of the drink had worn off. Therefore, nobody was really worried when Old Spider vanished from the scene completely. It was speculated that he had found a better chimney-space elsewhere. Some twenty years later, however, during renovations to the old "Bear Inn" the ostler of Stock was to make his reappearance, well blackened and equally well cured, his body being discovered jammed between the chimneys.

Many signs carry a lot of detail and are in fact works of art for they were executed by the leading artists of the day. In the old days these signs would stretch across the road from one building to another. At Wicken Bonhunt a finely detailed "Stagecoach and Horses" dominates the scene overlooking the innyard while at Colchester at "The George" a dandy walks a pug above the busy streaming traffic. At the little hamlet of Repentance, near Greenstead, where once wrongdoers worked in the fields as a "pennance" instead of going to prison, the inn sign at the "Drill" portrays one of the penitents at work.

Animal signs also prove interesting as "The Rabbits" at Stapleford Abbots and the "Kicking Dickey" at Great Dunmow portray. A rather special beast, the griffon was a protected animal as ancient manuscripts of the day remind us. This armorial bearing of the Spencer-Churchill family is to be found at the "Griffon Inn", Danbury. The "Lamb" of Ardleigh is hardly likely to be overlooked for this sign is in the form of a life-size jaunty lamb. The "Flying Fox" at Colchester could be the name of a flying squirrel although there was a famous race-horse of that name.

Signs which, because of their great numbers, get taken for granted but are still interesting for all that are in nearly every town and village. The "Black Boy" at Weeley and Wrabness is a sign which can be traced back to the 17th century when it was used extensively as a tobacconist's sign. A play on this sign is the "Black Buoy" at

The Roaring Donkey inn sign, a mockery of Napoleon, Holland-on-Sea

Wivenhoe, that ancient port where men like Phillip Sainty built ships capable of fast trips across the Channel in the days when smuggling was rife along this part of the coast. For the free-booter Sainty would build a ship complete with special compartments built into mast and keel to take those extra special little parcels that made a trip so worth while. For those who fell victim to the Excise men an inn with full meaning must surely be the "Hole-in-the-Wall" at Colchester. Thought to derive its name from the practice of slipping food and drink to prisoners held within the keep, the present inn is built into the Balkerne Wall high above the old guardroom.

Political overtones can also be found in some inn signs, for the "Goat in Boots" was a derisory term given to local rifle volunteers. After the Napoleonic Wars poor old Boney took a lot of ribbing usually being portrayed as a roaring donkey either in or out of a rowing boat. The "Roaring Donkey" at Holland-on-Sea is the nearest to this in Essex.

For a strictly county flavour the "Essex Skipper" inn at Maldon must surely be one of the best. Originally confined to just the county of Essex when it was first named in 1888 this butterfly is now countrywide, although owing to the widespread use of crop-sprays and general air pollution it, too, is facing extinction. A sign that caused

The Old Copper Kettle trade sign, Colchester

something of a stir when first hung is the "Angel" at Braintree. Depicting a winged angel complete with a foaming pint, both sport a halo which once made the local clergy protest loudly.

Signs which seem to have no background or explanation could be the "Wig and Fidgett" at Buxted and the "Bag of Nails" at Loughton. The latter could sometimes be seen accompanied with a picture of the Devil.

Trade signs, reflecting so vividly the calling of each business are rather scarce in Essex, many having been replaced by new-fangled electric or neon signs. Those that do exist are well cared for and despite numerous attempts of dealers or collectors to purchase them, are treasured as a kind of family heirloom.

The red and white striped barber's pole is now fast vanishing from the scene, being placed instead by an electrically operated plastic version. Originally the red pole served as a stand-fast for patients to grip while being bled, for the barber of those days also doubled as a surgeon. The white stripes denoted the bandages hung out to dry, while in the shop window one would have seen jars of leeches and sets of sharp blades known as fleams. One of the last remaining original barbers' poles can be seen at Manningtree.

Back once more in Colchester we find a large, blackened kettle and burner swinging above the cafe adjacent to the market at North Hill. In the days of horse transportation, market-goers had to rely on refreshments from the "Old Copper Kettle" or make-do with the nearby inn for more stronger beverages. On to Chelmsford and the gunsmiths of Leech & Son. In their small window we find on display a truly fine example of the gunsmith's art. This antique sporting gun is fitted with a rare Forsyth scent-bottle lock, one of the earliest known efficient methods of detonating a muzzle-loading weapon, using a fulminating mixture. Leech can also lay claim to perfecting a type of percussion revolver used by British officers during the Crimean campaign.

As many of the old original trade signs have been removed from shop fronts to make way for more modern, slim-line facias, a few interesting examples have taken their place inside the premises. A superb example of an 18th century carved wooden spinning-wheel in full working order can be found in the picturesque bow fronted window of Anne's Tea Rooms, Frinton. At Thorrington we find a wrought-iron gate which has the blacksmith's name and items of his trade incorporated into the design, making a most unusual trade sign. At Little Easton near Dunmow an old sign "The Laundry" swings and

Coal tax post on the road to Epping Forest

creaks on its rotting post. It is thought to be the trade sign of the laundry that served Easton Lodge, home of the former Countess of Warwick.

The old road signs take some finding now for these are slowly being decimated. One that has links with the old Coal Tax can be found at Theydon Bois and the road to Epping. These unique cast-iron posts bearing the City of London Arms marks the limit for an old toll on coals entering the metropolis. The duty was levied in Edward II's reign by the City of London on coal which was delivered in sacks also bearing the City Arms. The duties being levied at 4/- per tun of wine and 1d per ton of coal. The tax was finally repealed by an Act of Parliament in 1889.

Another interesting road sign is that found just north of the railway bridge in Carpenter's Road, Stratford. This shows the Arms of the Carpenter's Company responsible for the making of the road and estate and at the same time acting as a boundary sign for the Company.

Closely connected with trade signs are the ornaments to be found on walls. Many wall ornaments seem to stem from the fact that someone had acquired the odd item and had nowhere else to stick it except on the nearest wall. Such must have been the plight of a piece of Saxon sculptured stone of the pre-Conquest period discovered in 1911 built into the churchyard wall at Barking. Now preserved in St. Margaret's parish church Barking, it is thought to have been erected after the Danish defeat and to mark the restoration of the abbey about the year 970 by King Edgar and Archbishop Dunstan.

Two giant curiosities are the whalebones mounted either side of the front door of Valence House, Dagenham. Their origin seems to have been lost with the passing of time for nobody seems sure about where they came from. Local legend has it that they came from a former inn.

Links with the old gods are all around us and on the wall of High Easter Church is a carved face resembling a sun. Yet another excellent example is mounted on a garden wall at Great Barfield. Carved in sandstone the grimacing Sun-god measures 2 ft. in diameter. A number of these carvings have been observed in Essex and one should always be on the look-out for them as they turn up in the most unexpected places. Mainly they are linked with the soldier's god, Mithras which was brought to England by the invading Romans. Mithras was Sol Invictus, the sun, who always conquered darkness and renewed strength every morning. While he was god of light and truth, he was also the deity of vegetation and of increase, a prosperer of the good and destroyer of the bad, an enemy of evil spirits, a protector of souls, a

Carved sun on garden wall, Great Bardfield

Lion's head carved in wood, St. Osyth Priory gatehouse

redeemer, and a champion of armies and of heroes. It was for a long while one of the most powerful and widespread religions in the world and indeed with the decline of the Roman Empire and the advent of the more pious Christianity, its rules, sacraments and orders were 'borrowed' and transferred to suit the new religion.

The remains of a Mithraic temple can be seen in the grounds of Colchester Castle Museum.

In the gatehouse of St. Osyth Priory one will find a large wood carving (approximately 3 ft. in diameter), fixed to the wall. In the form of a lion's head its original purpose has also been lost with the passing of time. Not so the carved wooden speeding greyhound that is mounted on the outhouse of Brooke Villa, Old Road, Gt. Clacton. It is claimed that it was washed ashore after the ill-fated ship "Greyhound" had sunk taking the captain and his two teenage sons with her during the late 19th century.

Wall decorations in the form of parge-work – ornamental plaster-work – can be found on a lot of old houses around the county. One of the best examples is at the Sun Inn, Saffron Walden while the 16th century Crown House, Newport, sports pargetting, a big shell-hood and the date 1692. It was at this house that Nell Gwyn stayed while Charles II attended the Newmarket Races. Much of the old way of Essex life can be identified in the pargetting as many pieces are set out in a form of tableau. At the Sun Inn, mentioned above, we find connections with Oliver Cromwell for he stayed at this inn during his many travels around the country. A set of Delft tiles (now in the Saffron Walden museum), were discovered during alterations to the building. One of these bore the portrait of the Lord Protector. Yet another example of this decorative work is to be found on the old Garrison House, near the quay at Wivenhoe. Pargetting, mainly confined to East Anglia is believed to have been introduced by Dutch settlers.

Whilst searching for these wall ornaments it won't be long before you stumble across some of the old fire-marks executed in copper or lead. Known as either fire-marks or fire-plates these are usually found on old timbered or half-timbered properties. The history of these plates can be traced back to 1666. After the great Fire of London in that year parishes were required to supply and maintain their own fire brigades. Insurance companies of the time also ran their own brigades dressing their men in magnificent colourful uniforms. An added attraction of being a uniformed fireman was the fact that it saved you from the press gangs that prowled around every large port and town. Marks were originally made in lead but by 1780–1800 were manufactured in copper. The practice of fixing marks usually on the front of a building

The Crown House, Nell Gwyn's country house, Newport

on a wall or beam of the first floor – was continued right up to 1860. Much rivalry existed between the different brigades and those who rushed to a fire only to discover the burning dwelling bore another company's sign, would sometimes hinder their opponents by getting in the way of the manually operated fire-engine or tip over the rows of leather fire buckets. Often the house would burn to a crisp while a group of fighting, swearing firemen sorted out their differences in front of the roaring flames. Many old fire-marks have vanished completely but a choice example is mounted on a house in Trinity Street, Colchester, while, at Castle Hill, Dedham, we find another two plates one of them bearing a castellated tower.

Houses which sport corbels – those ornate pieces of stonemason's art – are well worth searching for as usually they have a story to tell. The carved head on a capitol in the church at Great Baddow tells its own tale for the scowling female wears a nag's bridle or scold. Another corbel at Hornchurch mounted on the church is carved in the form of a horned bull. Legend has it that the prior on his way to church was charged by a bull but was saved when a herd of cows surrounded him thus warding off the attack.

The Old Garrison House, Wivenhoe, showing a superb example of pargetting

Sun fire-mark, Trinity Street, Colchester

Closely associated with corbels are the carved house brackets usually found on the corners of ancient buildings. Known as the "Hag of Felsted" a carved bracket is to be found on the George Boote house, on the bressumer above the west front window. It was common practice to harness a figurehead (very much the same as a ship's figurehead), to a house to keep off evil spirits. This one, naked with bulging eyes, and cloven hooves, is harnessed with a chastity belt and carries the inscription "George Boote made mee 1594". For what reason George Boote chose such a grotesque creature to guard his home we shall never know, but legend has it that the "Hag" was in fact his wife. Another two, although these are only 17th century, can be seen on a house in the market square, Waltham Cross and on a farm known as Eyart's Farm, Terling.

One of the oldest forms of art are the stained glass windows which exist in great variety in churches around the country. Many carry legends that stretch back into history while others have links with happenings of just the past twenty to thirty years. Made from hundreds of pieces of coloured glass soldered into a lead frame, the actual window can take anything up to eight weeks to finish. One of the oldest windows in Essex is that of Robert Lemaire in the parish church at Rivenhall. Said to be of 13th century workmanship it depicts a knight in full armour. Another interesting example is that at Little Bromley Church. This depicts Charles I, the unhappy king who lost his head, and bears the legend "Charles Stuart, King and Martyr" A much more modern window is that in the porch of Chelmsford cathedral. Dedicated to the memory of members of the USAF who served and fell while stationed in Essex during World War II, it illustrates the role these men played during the war. All manner of subjects are to be found portrayed including the group of pigs shown feeding and a man sowing seeds. The feeding pigs are to be seen in the church at Margaretting while the husbandman is at Colne Engaine church.

The legend of St. George and the Dragon is one that is to be found all over Europe in one form or another but Essex can lay claim to fathering the English version. A visit to the parish church of Wormingford reveals an outstanding stained glass window with a St. George and Dragon motif. This and a nearby field rejoicing to the name of the "Bloody Meadow" sets the scene for an exciting legend.

In the reign of Richard I (1189-1199), after abandoning his third crusade, it is reported that the King brought back from the Holy Land a "curious little cokadrille". Once home in England he housed his new found pet in the Tower of London as a start to the royal menagerie,

"Hag of Felsted", a carved house bracket mounted on George Booke's house, 1594

Stained glass window, depicting Charles I, Little Bromley Church

Topiary bird in the grounds of St. Osyth Priory

which flourished until 1835. Although this strange beast was small to begin with once in London it seemed to thrive on the food and air so much that it soon grew to startling proportions and yearned for greener pastures. Breaking out of its cage it slipped off on an exploratory voyage down the river Thames. Finally it found its way inland and into the pleasant Essex countryside. Greener fields this "cokadrille" may have searched for but when the villagers of Withermundford – as it was then called – learned of the rampagings of King Richard's little pet they quite rightly panicked and proceeded to sacrifice a few virgins in an attempt to pacify the scaly monster. Finally they had to call upon their lord, Sir George de la Haye to rid them of the fiery beast. Taking up lance and armour the bold lord tracked down the dragon, cornering it near the river and after a one-sided struggle finally dispatched the strange beast. Sir George became a hero, and from then on the field was known as "Bloody Meadow".

Although many stories revolve around St. George and the Dragon, this one is the most popular version. As one of the villagers pointed out, "Our village became known as Warmyngford or Wermyngford soon after the incident and the first part of the name was an old term for serpent or dragon."

A window which can relate another poignant story although it is not in fact of stained glass, is the writing scratched into the glass at 126, High Street, Witham. Thought to have been written by a man awaiting the stage-coach to take him to prison it is dated 1740.

Abercrombie.

Stand on the funeral pile, immortal fame,
Broad stars adorn, they brightest robe,
The thousand voices round his name
In silver accents round the globe.
Glory, with all her lamps, shall burn,
To watch the warrior's sleeping clay,
Till the last trumpet rouse his urne
To aid the triumphs of the day!

Much research has gone into trying to indentify the author but to date it still remains one of our Essex curiosities and unsolved mysteries.

CHAPTER X

Topiary, Dovecotes, Show-Gardens, Mazes

Over the years many writers have labelled Essex as a flat and uninteresting county. Flat it may be but just how uninteresting can be judged by the past nine chapters . . . the churches, barns, houses, memorials, castles and gravestones all have a story to tell for those with the time to spare and the inclination to search and enquire. As you motor through the country lanes of Essex you can often find the odd garden or two which has had more than the usual care and attention lavished upon it. Often it is more noticeable or eye-catching for the added attraction of the well kept topiary work.

Topiary work is one of the oldest garden arts known having been started in ancient China. A glance at some of the fragile porcelain and cloisonne enamel work to be found in our museums and leading salerooms will readily verify this claim! The Romans were next to experiment with topiary for a leading gardener by the name of Toparius gained fame for constructing with great skill, ships, temples, birds and beasts out of the common ever-green trees and bushes.

Introduced into Britain by the Romans yew was a popular shrub which was to be seen clipped and shaped in all manner of odd designs outside Roman villas. During the Middle Ages with the upheaval of war and bloodshed, topiary almost died out. However, with the calming influence of Charles II it was reintroduced with full splendour at Hampton Court.

Out at Bartlow we find a large topiary train cleverly cut from the evergreen.

Not all the examples of topiary work are restricted to large show gardens for a few of our rural railway stations have the odd figure or two and compete in a friendly way to try and outdo each other with original designs. At Little Bardfield, at a house which was formerly the

The oldest tree in Essex, Gt. Yeldham

Chequers Inn, a very ornate piece of topiary can be seen while in the grounds of St. Osyth Priory a selection of evergreen birds can be seen vying dramatically with their live counterparts strutting majestically around the expansive lawns.

Forests and woodlands are slowly giving way to the advance of the developer, but a few still worth visiting can be found in the county of Essex. Epping Forest is all that remains of the Great Forest of Waltham, but that which remains offers the rambler a complete contrast. Here he can walk un-mapped footpaths for miles with crossing paths threading through the Forest, and with hornbeams, beeches, birches and oaks surrounding him wherever he walks. In the middle of the Forest is High Beech, which commands a fine view over Waltham Abbey.

In the churchyards we find many ancient yew trees which can trace their history back into the dark-ages. Yew, that magic wood which went to build the all-powerful longbow was a protected tree and consequently grown in the sanctity of a churchyard. The oldest tree to flourish in Essex is a giant oak tree, at Great Yeldham 30 feet in circumference, and held together with iron bands, rivets and all the wonders of modern tree-surgery. On top of Colchester Castle – the tower on the south-west angle – is a lone sycamore erected in commemoration of the victory at Waterloo, on June 18th, 1815.

Where trees abound birds are bound to gather so beneath the shade of the overhanging greenery we find the rather ornate dovecote which in olden times could be found on most large estates. Doves, being a very fine delicacy for both rich and poor alike had to be housed in a well-built, weather and vermin proof structure so we find those dovecotes that are still standing in a fair state of preservation. Many have gone the way of many interesting farm buildings having been utilised as tractor sheds or fertiliser stores but one that has escaped this fate is the dovecote to be found at the entrance of Guymer's Farm, Battlesbridge. It is thought to be late 18th or 19th century and bears the inscription "W.B. 1819" on the wooden door frame. Inside there is accommodation for some 600 birds which is a lot of birds by any standard. The heavy locking bar mounted on the door bears silent testimony to the fears of prowling poachers. At Sibley's Farm, Chickney, just south of the house we find a dovecote of timber framing and weather boarding; the roof being partly thatched and partly tiled. It has four bays with queen-post trusses of the 16th century.

Spains Hall, Finchingfield, home of Sir John Ruggles-Brise, Lord Lieutenant of Essex

Martin's Farm, Newport. Remains of a 16th century dovecote in the roof.

Dynes Hall, Great Maplestead. The pigeon-house lies south-west of the stables being timber-framed and plastered, and has pyramidal tiled roof gables at the apex. It was built around 1600.

Place Farm, Elsenham, A 17th century, square, timber-framed and plastered dovecote to be found at the rear of the house.

Woolpits Farm, Bardfield Saling, being square and built of red brick; the roof is pyramidal with a timber lantern or cot.

Great Bardfield Hall, This dovecot, built on the south side of the Hall, is square, timber-framed and plastered, and has a tiled pyramidal roof with a lantern. Probably of 17th century construction.

Oldbourne's Farm, Finchingfield. Pigeon-house built of brick and has a timber lantern in the middle. Last used as a stable. The walls have a moulded plinth and string course, and three windows are each of two lights with moulded jambs, mullions and labels.

Essex is also renowned for its famous roses and many of the picturesque gardens scattered around the county are thrown open to the public during the summer months as a kind of shop window. Many of these show-gardens can be traced back over the centuries when rich lords and ladies lavished small fortunes designing and laying out their show-places. Many of the plants and trees were brought back in the holds of returning East Indiamen as they sailed around the newly won colonies – shades of H.M.S. Bounty and Captain Bligh! – while others were nurtured with great care by the faithful head-gardeners.

Some are of fairly modern construction being only some 20 to 30 years old on land reclaimed after the "Dig for Victory" fervour during World War Two. Quite a number of these show gardens can be visited on payment of a small fee. Entrance times differ from month to month and garden to garden while some include a visit to an interesting house though not all. It is far better to enquire beforehand asking for full details, and a prompt reply will be guaranteed if a stamped addressed envelope is included.

Rickling House, Quendon. Medium-sized garden; good collection species roses, daffodils, peonies, lilies and flowering shrubs. On A.11 6 miles south of Saffron Walden.

Gun Hill Place, Dedham. 5 miles north-east of Colchester. Flower gardens, spring bulbs, azaleas, rhododendrons, oaks, cedars, beeches, Spanish chestnuts, specimen trees and a fine lake.

Terling Place, Terling, north-east of Chelmsford between A12 and A.131. Spring flowering bulbs and shrubs. Formal garden of clipped yew, roses, many coniferous trees. The house built in 1772; wings added in 1818. Architect: John Johnson.

Theydon Priory, Theydon Bois, south of Epping and north of the A.113. Good selection of bulbs, flowering trees, shrubs, walled garden.

Moat House, Great Easton, Dunmow. Modern garden of 3½ acres. Water garden, pond with "willow pattern" bridge leading to an island and a temple. 4½ miles from Thaxted on the A.130, just 3 miles from Great Dunmow.

Hedingham Castle, near Halstead, primulas and fine flowering shrubs as well as the Norman Keep which we have already covered in chapter three. 4 miles north of Halstead off A.604.

Brizes Park, Kelvedon Hatch, north-west of Brentwood on the A.128. Medium-sized garden and a walled kitchen garden. Also a park. A fine 18th century house built in 1722 dominates the whole scene but it is not open to the public.

New Farm, Great Easton, North of Dunmow. Modern Garden; flowering trees, shrubs, rock garden, old oak and other trees.

Spains Hall, Finchingfield. North-west of Braintree and west of the B.1057. Home of Sir John Ruggles-Brise, Lord Lieutenant of Essex. Fine Elizabethan house. Garden set out with a select display of roses and herbaceous borders.

Colne Place, Earls Colne, north-west of Colchester on the A.604. Clipped yew and holly hedges, 17 ft. high, surrounds main portion of garden. Herbaceous border, delphiniums, lilies, annuals.

Le Pavilon, Newport. From A.11 turn right at lodge north of Newport. Medium-sized garden; herbaceous and shrub borders; roses; greenhouses.

Park Lodge, Margaretting. North-east of Ingatestone on the A.12. Small garden with a small collection of wild fowl. Budgerigars flying at liberty.

Durrington House, 1 mile north-east of old Harlow. Medium sized garden with large lawns and fine trees; roses and herbaceous borders, two ponds, a walled kitchen garden and green houses. Set amidst this is a superb 18th century house (not open to the public).

Kelvedon Hall, north-west of Brentwood on the A.128. Botanically interesting with a walled rose garden, yew hedges, mixed borders and a lily pond.

Great Chalks, Hatfield Broad Oak, near Bishop's Stortford. Two acres with sloping lawns, fine trees, a great variety of shrubs and a small pool and alpine bed. On the B.183 Hatfield Heath – Takelet Road.

Hill Pasture, Broxted, near Dunmow on the B.1051 near junction of Dunmow – Thaxted road. Thaxted 3½ miles, Dunmow 5 miles. A modern romantic landscape garden, illustrated in *Country Life* magazine. Lily pond, moongate and a temple set in 3 acres surrounded by shrubs and old-fashioned roses.

Clavering Court, Clavering. Three acres of well laid out gardens with magnificent copper beech and Wellingtonia; shrubs and herbaceous border with rosebeds and lawns, also a good selection of statuary.

East Hall, Mersea Island, just 10 miles south of Colchester. Five acres of gardens made-up of lawns, young specimen trees, shrubs, herbaceous borders, etc., set in a moated area together with a Tudor house.

Little Garretts, North End. Four miles south of Great Dunmow. A medium-sized garden and quite outstanding, having a fair amount of livestock including capuchin monkeys, and goats and sheep which have been conditioned to accept the attentions of children.

Waltons, Ashdon. About ½ mile east of Saffron Walden – Bartlow Road. Fine selection of roses, walled kitchen garden and herbaceous borders, flowering shrubs.

White Barn House, Elmstead Market. Leave Colchester on A.133 for Clacton through Elmstead Market. Three acres of attractively landscaped garden with many unusual plants shown in a wide range of conditions from hot and dry to the water garden.

Gubbions Hall, Great Leighs. Well laid out garden surrounded by ancient 19th century moat with ornamental ducks; flowering trees and shrubs. Also 20 acres of woodland through which visitors may stroll.

The White House, Riffham's Chase, Little Baddow. Just three miles east of Chelmsford. A medium-sized garden; magnificent trees; oaks of great age; arbutus; rhododendrons, azaleas, camellias, roses, herbaceous borders.

Wickham Hall, Wickham Bishops. South-east of Witham and east of B.1018 Langford – Witham Road. Spring flowers, rockery and a Queen Anne house (moated).

The Old Rectory, Lawford, near Manningtree, on the A.604 Colchester – Harwich Road. Three acres of garden spread out on edge of Dedham Vale. Herbaceous borders, fine trees, evergreens and an orchard.

Although not open to the public, a visit to Bridge End, Saffron Walden, will prove well worth while just to view the splendid Dutch Garden.

Mazes have always been quite fascinating and legend has it that they were originally built as a punishment for penitents in the middle-ages. Led into the middle and left alone the wrong-doer could reflect upon his misdeeds whilst attempting to find his way out of the close-knit, winding pathways. An unusual example is to be found cut in the turf on the common at Saffron Walden which consists of a series of concentric circles. The origin of the work is doubtful, but there is evidence that the maze was re-cut in 1699 at the cost of 15/- which was a lot of money in that day and age.

BIBLIOGRAPHY

ESSEX GHOSTS – The Haunted Towns and Villages of Essex. James Wentworth-Day, Spur 1974.

WITCHCRAFT IN ESSEX, Glyn H. Morgan, Spur 1974.

ESSEX CRAFTS, S. Jarvis and C. Harrison, Spur 1974.

SHORT WALKS IN SOUTH ESSEX, Frank Dawes, Illustrated by Leonard Wyatt, Spur 1974.

THE ROMANCE OF ESSEX INNS, Glyn H. Morgan, Spur 1974.

COUNTRY CURIOSITIES, Raymond Lea, Spur 1974.

INDEX

INDEX

Printed in Great Britain by Compton Printing Ltd.
London and Aylesbury.

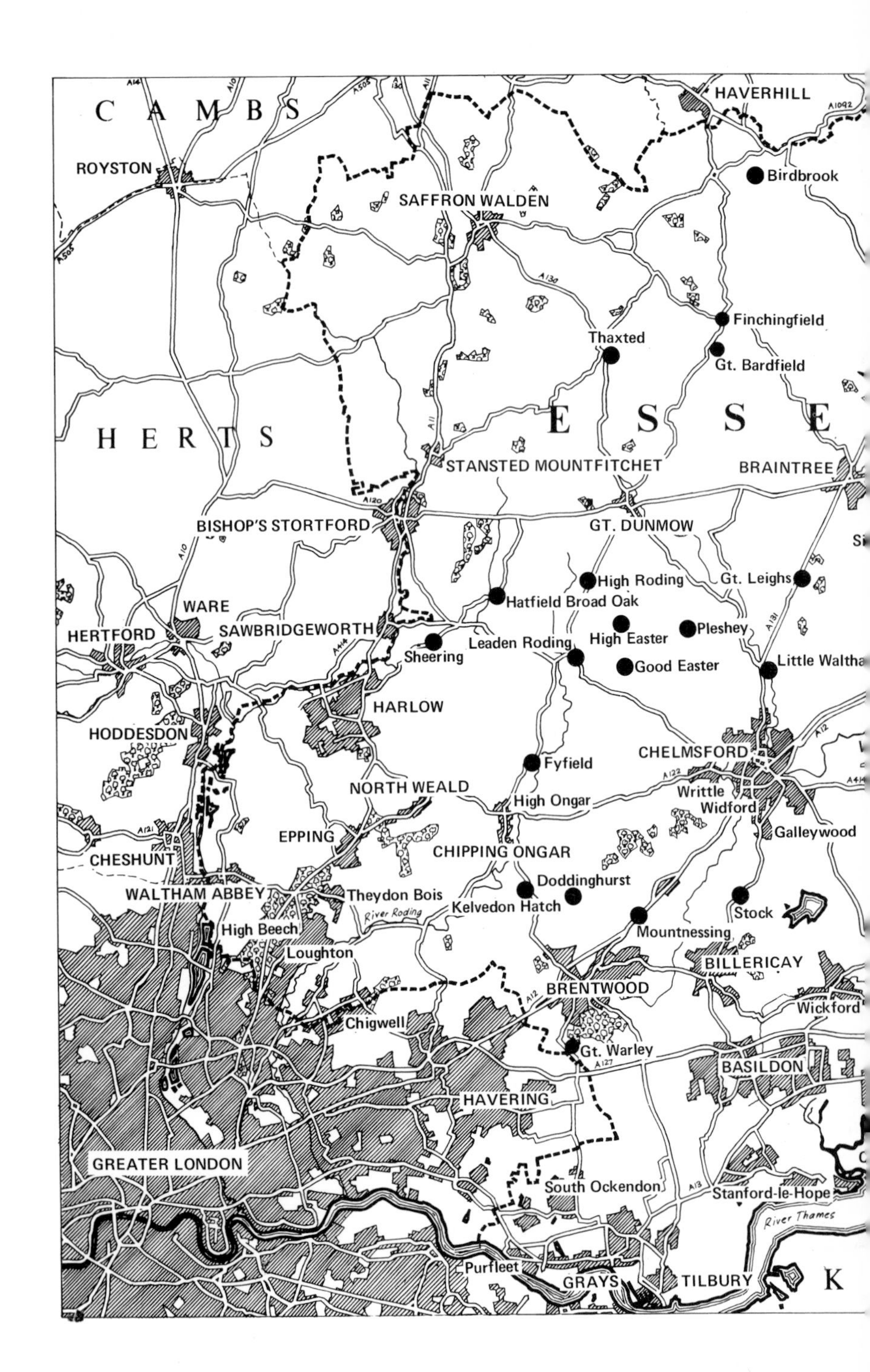
CAMBS
HERTS
ESSEX
ROYSTON
HAVERHILL
Birdbrook
SAFFRON WALDEN
Finchingfield
Thaxted
Gt. Bardfield
STANSTED MOUNTFITCHET
BRAINTREE
BISHOP'S STORTFORD
GT. DUNMOW
High Roding
Gt. Leighs
Hatfield Broad Oak
WARE
HERTFORD
SAWBRIDGEWORTH
Pleshey
High Easter
Sheering
Leaden Roding
Good Easter
Little Waltha
HARLOW
HODDESDON
CHELMSFORD
Fyfield
NORTH WEALD
High Ongar
Writtle
Widford
EPPING
Galleywood
CHESHUNT
CHIPPING ONGAR
Doddinghurst
WALTHAM ABBEY
Theydon Bois
Kelvedon Hatch
Stock
River Roding
High Beech
Mountnessing
Loughton
BILLERICAY
BRENTWOOD
Wickford
Chigwell
Gt. Warley
BASILDON
HAVERING
GREATER LONDON
South Ockendon
Stanford-le-Hope
River Thames
Purfleet
GRAYS
TILBURY
K
A14
A10
A505
A11
A120
A414
A121
A130
A12
A127
A13
A131
A122
A1092